Mirza Ghazanfar Beg
Mohammad Faisal
Sandeep Kumar Nayak

Advancing Pandemic Prediction With Big Data and Machine Learning

Mirza Ghazanfar Beg
Mohammad Faisal
Sandeep Kumar Nayak

Advancing Pandemic Prediction With Big Data and Machine Learning

Early Pandemic Prediction with Big Data: Unified Approach Using Supervised & Unsupervised Learning

LAP LAMBERT Academic Publishing

Imprint
Any brand names and product names mentioned in this book are subject to trademark, brand or patent protection and are trademarks or registered trademarks of their respective holders. The use of brand names, product names, common names, trade names, product descriptions etc. even without a particular marking in this work is in no way to be construed to mean that such names may be regarded as unrestricted in respect of trademark and brand protection legislation and could thus be used by anyone.

Cover image: www.ingimage.com

Publisher:
LAP LAMBERT Academic Publishing
is a trademark of
Dodo Books Indian Ocean Ltd. and OmniScriptum S.R.L publishing group

120 High Road, East Finchley, London, N2 9ED, United Kingdom
Str. Armeneasca 28/1, office 1, Chisinau MD-2012, Republic of Moldova, Europe
Managing Directors: Ieva Konstantinova, Victoria Ursu
info@omniscriptum.com

Printed at: see last page
ISBN: 978-620-8-42055-0

Advancing Pandemic Prediction with Big Data and Machine Learning

(Early Pandemic Prediction with Big Data: Unified Approach Using Supervised & Unsupervised Learning)

TABLE OF CONTENT

LIST OF TABLES

LIST OF FIGURES

LIST OF ABBREVIATION

AHP	:	Analytic Hierarchy Process
AI	:	Artificial Intelligence
API	:	Application Programming Interface
AR	:	Augmented Reality
CCPA	:	California Consumer Privacy Act
CNN	:	Convolutional Neural Network
FN	:	False Negative
FP	:	False Positive
GAN	:	Generative Adversarial Network
GDPR	:	General Data Protection Regulation
GMM	:	Gaussian Mixture Models
GPS	:	Global Positioning System
HDFS	:	Hadoop Distributed File System
IoT	:	Internet of Things
JSON	:	Java Script object Notation
LDA	:	Linear Discriminant Analysis
LOF	:	Local Outlier Factor
MAE	:	Mean Absolute Error
MCDM	:	Multi-Criteria Decision-Making
ML	:	Machine Learning
MSE	:	Mean Squared Error
NLP	:	Natural Language Processing
PCA	:	Principal Component Analysis
RMSLE	:	Root Mean Squared Logarithmic Error
RNN	:	Recurrent Neural Network
ROC	:	Receiver Operating Characteristic
SAW	:	Simple Additive Weighting
SEIQR	:	Susceptibility Exposure Infection Quarantine Death Recovery
SIR	:	Susceptible Infectious Recovered or Removed
SL	:	Supervised Learning
SQL	:	Structure Query Learning
SVM	:	Support Vector Machine
TN	:	True Negative
TP	:	True Positive
UL	:	Unsupervised Learning
VAE	:	Variational Autoencoder
VR	:	Virtual Reality
WHO	:	World Health Organization
XML	:	Markup Learning
YARN	:	Yet Another Resource Negotiator

ABSTRACT

Data science and artificial intelligence have been altered by the discipline of big data engineering, advancing systems and allowing for the creation of better technologies. These technologies are used by engineers to create products that improve our comprehension of physical events. A key component in transforming this technology to improve the world is machine learning (ML). Designing interactive machines is made possible by approaches and strategies built into machine learning (ML) technologies. The performance of supervised and unsupervised machine learning algorithms for illness prediction is the main topic of this study's survey of ML applications in Mechanical Data Engineering. Researchers can choose the best supervised machine learning algorithm for their studies by being aware of the relative performance of various algorithms. Data mining has made extensive use of supervised machine learning techniques, and one possible application area is illness prediction utilizing health data. In order to forecast illness risk, this study intends to discover significant trends in the performance of supervised and unsupervised machine learning systems.

To tackle emerging illnesses and get ready for pandemics in the digital age, healthcare delivery needs the backing of cutting-edge technologies like artificial intelligence (AI), the internet of things (IoT), big data, and machine learning. This paper investigates the importance of AI as a tool for data analysis, illness prevention, and pandemic preparedness. Forecasting techniques based on machine learning have demonstrated their value in predicting postoperative outcomes and enhancing decision-making. In several fields, ML models have been widely utilized to categories and rank negative aspects for possible risks. In order to estimate the increase rate of COVID infections, this study suggests a hybrid machine learning technique for pandemic prediction that may be an effective substitute for SIR-based models. The proposed strategy can also enhance early detection of outbreaks.

Currently, a wide range of epidemiological models are used to forecast pandemic death rates and individual infections. However, because there is a dearth of pertinent, trustworthy, and important data, only a small number of models are able to produce prompt and precise choices. Huge amounts of data are processed and stored in numerous formats in the present era of digitization. This data must be thoroughly analysed and structured since it contains both operational and non-operational information. Unsupervised learning is useful for finding equally likely entities for potential future scenarios, but supervised learning may be used to extract data requirements from labelled data. This study uses a suggested method for unsupervised analysis of large amounts of movie data to find equally likely items. Incorporating the most recent developments in Artificial Intelligence and Machine Learning, such as Deep Learning, Graphical Models, and Reinforcement Learning, the research focuses on effective methodologies such as Unsupervised Learning Data and Supervised Learning Data. In order to comprehend the behavioral influence on data science, the task entails intensive observation of massive datasets and Big Data analysis. The major goal of the proposed study is to create a Big Data prediction method from both an unsupervised and supervised learning standpoint.

Data science is the process of drawing conclusions from data and using analysis to solve business problems. It includes the study of data storage strategies, data analysis processes, and data visualization methods. Data science incorporates math, stats, programming, methods to problem-solving, data acquisition capabilities, and activities for data preparation and cleaning. It is a multidisciplinary area that includes Big Data Technology, Artificial Intelligence, Machine Learning, Analytics, Statistics, and Mathematics. The complexity of data mining is still not fully understood, despite the fact that machine learning and data mining have been active study topics for decades. Recent work suggests using data science to problems involving dynamically served data. In order to overcome the obstacles posed by Big Data Analytics at the data model and system levels, high-performance computing platforms and methodical architectures are needed. Information analysis problems may be solved while supplying an abstract, highly secure, scalable, and affordable platform by using Unsupervised and Supervised Learning approaches to find outliers and unfitting data.

Data preparation, analysis, and cleaning are all included in data science. Applying cutting-edge analytical methods to sizable datasets in order to uncover and utilize business insights is known as big data analytics. Larger datasets, however, are more challenging to manage. Data Science combines activities like data mining, data analysis, mathematics, statistics, information technology, computer programming, data engineering, pattern recognition, visualization, and high-performance computing to effectively manage large volumes of data to extract meaningful and coherent results. A thorough review of several Data Science tools is given in this paper.

Data Science is a multidisciplinary discipline that includes Big Data Technology, Artificial Intelligence, Machine Learning, Statistics, Mathematics, and Statistics. Despite the fact that machine learning (data mining and analysis) has been a focus of active study for a few decades, the complexity of data mining is still not fully appreciated. The use of data science to address the problems associated with processing dynamically served data has been suggested in recent research. Several obstacles exist at the data model and system levels for big data analytics.

High-performance computing platforms and methods are necessary to enable big data analytics because they enforce systematic architectures that let big data run free. In addition to addressing the problem of information analysis, using supervised and unsupervised learning to identify outliers and data unfitness's also offer an abstract, highly secure, scalable, and economical platform for the suggested task.

Chapter 1:

Introduction and Motivation

1.1 Background

The era of today is characterized by a constant presence of data, permeating every aspect of daily life. While the three traditional states of matters are solid, liquid, and gas, the world finds itself surrounded by an informational cloud, where data exists as a ubiquitous entity. In fact, the term "Big Data" has emerged to describe the trail of data left behind as people navigate through the world.

Whether it is through text messages, social media posts, or simply walking in a city, different antennas and GPS systems continuously capture and collect data, creating a constant stream of Big Data. People may not even be aware of it, but a constant generation and leaving behind of digital residue occur. In this digital age, it has become imperative to be mindful of the Big Data generated and strive to minimize its impact.

This reality reflects the exponential growth of data on time. Let us delve into the historical context of this phenomenon and understand how it has shaped human existence. In the current era of digitalization, vast amounts of data are processed and stored in various formats. These voluminous datasets can be categorized as operational or non-operational, depending on their purpose (Wiggins, 2023). Regular transitions and operations necessitate the continuous analysis and structuring of such data. Meanwhile, the deposition of past data serves as a valuable resource for future endeavors.

Data specification can be accomplished through supervised learning, where labeled data assists in extracting relevant information. On the other hand, unsupervised learning techniques are employed to identify equally likely entities for future prospects. This research aims to identify various equally likely items through an unsupervised approach using voluminous movie data.

The term "big data" refers to extensive and intricate datasets that surpass the capacity of traditional data processing tools to manage. These datasets originate from diverse sources such as social media, mobile devices, sensors, and more. The primary challenge posed by big data lies in effectively processing and analyzing it to extract meaningful patterns, trends, and insights, enabling better decision-making.

When discussing big data, the three V's—volume, velocity, and variety—are often associated with it. The volume of data generated is immense, encompassing various formats such as text, images, videos, and audio. The velocity at which data is generated is high, as it flows in real-time from multiple sources. Additionally, the variety of data generated is extensive, comprising unstructured, semi-structured, and structured data.

Machine learning, a subset of Artificial Intelligence (AI), plays a significant role in handling big data. It enables computers to learn from data, identify patterns, and improve performance without explicit programming. The concept is rooted in the idea that machines can autonomously learn, make decisions, and derive insights from vast amounts of data without human intervention (Elavarasan et al., 2021).

In the realm of big data, the introduction and motivation serve a vital purpose similar to other fields, but with a specific focus on the challenges and opportunities presented by large and complex datasets. The introduction provides a background on the evolution of data collection, storage, and analysis, emphasizing the exponential growth in data volume, variety, and velocity over the past few decades. This context helps readers comprehend why big data has emerged as a significant field of study, accompanied by its unique challenges and opportunities.

The motivation for studying big data and data science lies in the potential benefits of analyzing massive datasets to gain insights into complex systems and phenomena (Sangaiah, 2019). Examples include understanding disease outbreaks, consumer behaviors, or climate change patterns. Conversely, motivation can also stem from the challenges associated with managing, processing, and analyzing vast amounts of data, as well as the risks posed by relying on faulty or biased analysis. Both aspects of motivation lay the groundwork for the subsequent content, providing context and establishing the key questions or issues that will be addressed. Moreover, they emphasize the importance and relevance of big data as an exciting field of study with broad applications across various industries.

1.2 Research Context

In the past few years, the proliferation of digital information has led to the advent of the big data era. This transformative phase is characterized by the generation and accumulation of vast amounts of data at an unprecedented pace. These datasets, known as big data, are diverse and intricate, necessitating sophisticated methodologies for effective analysis and extraction of valuable insights. Among the many applications of big data analytics, prediction stands out as a critical component in comprehending patterns, facilitating informed decision-making, and optimizing various processes. Hence, the development of precise and efficient prediction techniques holds immense significance in unlocking the full potential of big data.

The emergence of big data has revolutionized the way organizations operate and make decisions. With the ever-increasing volume and variety of data sources, traditional methods of data analysis and prediction have become insufficient. The sheer magnitude of information available demands innovative approaches that can handle the complexity and scale of big data (Wiggins, 2023). Prediction, in the context of big data analytics, involves forecasting future outcomes or trends based on historical data patterns. It enables organizations to anticipate potential developments, identify opportunities, mitigate risks, and optimize resource allocation. By leveraging advanced analytics techniques, such as machine learning and artificial intelligence, prediction models can be trained to uncover hidden patterns, correlations, and dependencies within large and diverse datasets.

Accurate prediction in the realm of big data is a challenging task due to several factors. Firstly, the volume of data is immense, making it difficult to process and analyze using traditional methods. Secondly, the velocity at which data is generated necessitates real-time or near-real-time prediction capabilities to keep up with the dynamic nature of the data. Thirdly, the variety of data types, including structured, unstructured, and semi-structured data, adds complexity to the prediction process (Omar & Sukthankar, 2023). Lastly, the veracity of data, encompassing issues such as data quality, reliability, and uncertainty, further complicates prediction tasks.

To address these challenges, researchers and practitioners have been actively exploring various prediction techniques tailored for big data analytics. One popular approach is machine learning, which involves training algorithms on large datasets to recognize patterns and make accurate predictions (Avdiukhin et al., 2019). Machine learning algorithms, such as decision trees, random forests, support vector machines, and neural networks, have shown promise in handling big data prediction tasks (Silaparasetty, 2020). These algorithms can automatically learn from the data, adapt to changing patterns, and make predictions with high accuracy.

Deep learning, a subset of machine learning, has gained significant attention in recent years for its ability to effectively process and analyze large-scale datasets. Deep neural networks, with their multiple layers of interconnected nodes, excel at capturing complex relationships and patterns in big data. By leveraging deep learning architectures, researchers have achieved breakthroughs in various domains, including image recognition, natural language processing, and time series prediction (Ledziński & Grześk, 2023).

In addition to machine learning and deep learning techniques, ensemble methods have emerged as powerful tools for big data prediction. Ensemble methods combine multiple models to generate more robust and accurate predictions (Silaparasetty, 2020). By aggregating the predictions of individual models, ensemble methods can overcome limitations and biases of individual models, leading to improved prediction performance.

Furthermore, advancements in distributed computing and parallel processing have enabled the implementation of scalable prediction algorithms that can efficiently handle big data. Distributed frameworks, such as Apache Hadoop and Apache Spark, facilitate the distributed processing of data across clusters of computers, enabling faster and more efficient prediction tasks on large datasets. These frameworks provide fault tolerance, scalability, and high-performance capabilities, making them well-suited for big data analytics.

In conclusion, the era of big data has brought about unprecedented challenges and opportunities for organizations across various industries. The ability to accurately predict future outcomes and trends based on massive and diverse datasets is crucial for making informed decisions and gaining a competitive edge. Through the application of advanced analytics techniques, such as machine learning, deep learning, ensemble methods, and distributed computing, researchers and practitioners are striving to develop efficient and accurate prediction models tailored for big data analytics (Gulve et al., 2023). As big data continues to expand, the development of robust prediction techniques will play a pivotal role in unlocking the full potential of this vast resource.

1.3 Problem Statement

The problem statement addressed in this research is the requirement for robust prediction techniques capable of handling the complexities and scale of big data (Löfström, 2009). Traditional prediction approaches may not be suitable for big data due to the enormous size of the datasets, high dimensionality, and the presence of noise and outliers. Additionally, the dynamic nature of big data necessitates adaptive and scalable techniques that can process data in real-time or near-real-time. Therefore, there is an urgent need to develop prediction techniques that can effectively harness the potential of big data and provide accurate predictions in a timely manner.

The rapid growth of big data presents significant challenges in terms of scalability, complexity, and heterogeneity, rendering traditional prediction techniques inadequate. While both unsupervised and supervised learning approaches have shown promise in addressing these challenges, there is a need for the development of novel prediction techniques that can leverage the benefits of both approaches within the context of big data. This book aims to bridge this gap by proposing and evaluating a prediction technique that combines unsupervised and supervised learning perspectives, specifically tailored for big data analysis.

Machine learning has emerged as an indispensable tool for solving a wide range of problems across various industries (Caindoy et al, 2016). However, several challenges and problems in the field of machine learning still need to be addressed. In this book, it will discuss some of the major problem statements in machine learning.

1.3.1 Lack of Quality Data: The success of machine learning models relies on the quality of the data they are trained on. However, obtaining high-quality data is often challenging. Data can be incomplete, noisy, or biased, which can adversely affect the model's performance. Addressing this problem requires the development of methods for cleaning and preprocessing data to ensure its high quality. Techniques such as data augmentation, data balancing, and outlier detection can be employed. It also requires methods for identifying and correcting biases in the data.

1.3.2 Overfitting and Underfitting: Overfitting occurs when a machine learning model is overly complex, resulting in high accuracy on the training data but poor performance on new, unseen data. Underfitting, on the other hand, occurs when a model is too simple and fails to capture the complexity of the data. Addressing this problem necessitates the development of methods for selecting appropriate model complexity that balances the bias-variance trade-off. Techniques such as cross-validation, regularization, and early stopping can be employed.

1.3.3 Lack of Explainability and Interpretability: Machine learning models are often considered as black boxes, making it challenging to understand how they make predictions. This lack of interpretability and explainability is a significant problem, particularly in critical applications such as healthcare and finance (Baig & Nayak, 2019). Addressing this problem requires the development of interpretable and explainable machine learning models. This can involve developing rule-based models that are easily understood and interpreted by humans, as well as visualization techniques that help understand the behavior of the model.

1.3.4 Data Privacy and Security: The use of machine learning models necessitates access to large amounts of data, raising concerns about privacy and security. Sensitive information such as personal identification, health, and financial data must be protected from unauthorized access. Addressing this problem requires the development of methods for preserving data privacy and security while still allowing the development of accurate machine learning models. Techniques such as differential privacy, federated learning, and homomorphic encryption can be employed.

1.3.5 Scalability and Efficiency: Machine learning models can require significant computational resources, making it challenging to scale them to large datasets or deploy them in resource-constrained environments. Addressing this problem requires the development of methods for improving the scalability and efficiency of machine learning models (Wiggins, 2023). This can involve developing distributed computing frameworks, optimizing algorithms, and utilizing hardware acceleration.

1.3.6 Model Selection and Evaluation: Machine learning models can be complex, with many hyperparameters that need to be tuned to achieve high performance (Ledziński & Grześk, 2023). Selecting the appropriate model and hyperparameters can be challenging, and evaluating model performance can be subjective. Addressing this problem requires the development of methods for selecting appropriate models and hyperparameters suitable for the task. Techniques such as grid search, Bayesian optimization, and model ensemble can be employed. It also requires the development of objective evaluation metrics that can be used to compare models across different tasks and datasets.

In conclusion, while machine learning has made significant advancements in recent years, there are still several problems that need to be addressed (Agalya et al., 2018). Overcoming these problems requires a multidisciplinary approach involving experts from computer science, statistics, and other relevant fields. By working together, can overcome these challenges and unlock the full potential of machine learning.

1.4 Research Objectives

The approve objective of this study is to develop a prediction technique in the context of big data analytics (Sangaiah, 2019). Specifically, the research aims to achieve the following objectives:

- Identify the existing models for Unsupervised and Supervised Learning of Data.
- Quantify the efficiency of existing models for Supervised Learning and Unsupervised Learning of Big Data.

    i. Study and Identify criteria of Big Data and study HDFS, MapReduce and YARN.
    ii. Issues and Challenges in Master-Slave Architecture of Big Data.
    iii. Quantify the efficiency of an existing model of Unsupervised Learning for Big Data.
    iv. Quantify the efficiency of an existing model of Supervised Learning for Big Data.

- Develop a hybrid Architecture and Technique for both Supervised Learning and Unsupervised Learning of Big Data.
- To Implement and Validate the developed proposed prediction technique.

By achieving these objectives, this research intends to contribute to the field of big data analytics by advancing the state-of-the-art in prediction techniques. The developed hybrid prediction technique has the potential to enable organizations to make accurate predictions from big data, leading to improved decision-making, enhanced operational efficiency, and competitive advantage in the data-driven era.

The research objective of this study is to identify and evaluate existing models for both unsupervised and supervised learning of data. Specifically, the efficiency of these models in handling big data will be quantified. Additionally, the study aims to explore the criteria of big data and examine the relation to big data processing (Elavarasan et al., 2021). The challenges and issues in the master-slave architecture of big data will also be investigated.

1.4.1 Explore Unsupervised Learning Perspective: The first objective is to investigate and analyze the potential of unsupervised learning algorithms for prediction in big data. Unsupervised learning techniques, such as clustering and anomaly detection, have the advantage of discovering patterns and relationships in data without the need for labeled training examples. The research will delve into the applicability, strengths, and limitations of unsupervised learning methods in predicting outcomes from big data.

1.4.2 Examine Unsupervised and Supervised Learning Perspective: The second objective is to examine the effectiveness of supervised learning algorithms for prediction in big data. Supervised learning techniques, such as classification and regression, leverage labeled training data to build predictive models. This objective involves studying various supervised learning algorithms and assessing their performance in the context of big data prediction. The research will explore the scalability, adaptability and accuracy of supervised learning approaches.

1.4.3 Develop Hybrid Prediction Technique: The third objective is to propose and develop a hybrid prediction technique that combines the strengths of unsupervised and supervised learning perspectives. This hybrid approach aims to leverage the advantages of both paradigms to enhance prediction accuracy, handle the challenges of big data, and address limitations present in individual techniques. The research will focus on developing novel algorithms and methodologies that integrate unsupervised and supervised learning techniques.

1.4.4 Evaluate and Validate the Prediction Technique: The fourth objective is to rigorously evaluate and validate the developed prediction technique. This involves conducting extensive experiments using real-world big data sets and benchmarking the performance against existing prediction methods. The research will employ appropriate evaluation metrics and statistical analyses to assess the accuracy, scalability, and efficiency of the proposed technique. Additionally, the research aims to validate the generalizability and robustness of the technique across different domains and datasets.

1.4.5 Provide Insights and Recommendations: The final objective is to provide valuable insights, recommendations, and guidelines for the practical implementation of the developed prediction technique in real-world scenarios. The research aims to offer actionable recommendations for organizations seeking to leverage big data for prediction purposes. These recommendations may include considerations related to data preprocessing, feature selection, model deployment, and scalability.

In conclusion, the research objective of this study encompasses various aspects, including the identification and evaluation of existing models for unsupervised and supervised learning of data, quantifying the efficiency of these models in the context of big data, exploring the criteria and frameworks associated with big data, addressing challenges in the master-slave architecture, and developing a hybrid architecture and technique for big data analysis (Amirian et al, 2017). The implementation and validation of the proposed technique will provide insights into its effectiveness and potential contributions to the field of big data analytics.

1.5 Significance and Motivation

Moreover, the dynamic nature of big data requires adaptive techniques that can handle real-time or near-real-time processing (Bhushan & Agarwal,2023). Traditional prediction approaches may struggle to keep up with the pace at which data is generated and require significant computational resources. By developing a prediction technique specifically tailored for big data analysis, this research aims to address these challenges and provide a solution that is scalable, efficient, and capable of producing accurate predictions in a timely manner.

The significance of this research lies in its potential to advance the field of big data analytics and machine learning. By combining unsupervised and supervised learning perspectives, the proposed technique can provide a holistic approach to analyzing and extracting insights from complex and diverse datasets. This can lead to a deeper understanding of patterns, trends, and relationships within the data, enabling better decision-making and improving various processes.

In industries such as finance, accurate predictions are crucial for detecting fraudulent activities and minimizing financial risks. By developing a robust prediction technique, this research can contribute to the development of more effective fraud detection systems, helping organizations safeguard their assets and protect against financial losses (Patel-Schneider et al, 2010).

In the healthcare domain, accurate predictions can aid in disease diagnosis and treatment planning. By analyzing large volumes of patient data, the proposed technique can assist healthcare professionals in identifying patterns and risk factors associated with various diseases. This can lead to early detection, timely interventions, and improved patient outcomes.

In marketing and customer behavior analysis, accurate predictions can enable organizations to understand consumer preferences, anticipate market trends, and tailor their strategies accordingly. By leveraging big data, the proposed technique can provide valuable insights into customer behavior, enabling businesses to optimize their marketing campaigns, improve customer satisfaction, and drive sales growth.

In the transportation industry, accurate predictions can help optimize traffic flow, reduce congestion, and improve overall transportation efficiency. By analyzing real-time data from various sources such as sensors, GPS devices, and traffic cameras, the proposed technique can provide timely predictions and recommendations for traffic management, route planning, and resource allocation.

Furthermore, the development of a prediction technique that combines unsupervised and supervised learning approaches can contribute to the advancement of machine learning as a whole. It can provide a framework for researchers and practitioners to explore new avenues in data analysis, knowledge discovery, and predictive modeling. This can lead to the development of more innovative and effective machine learning algorithms and techniques, benefiting various fields beyond big data analytics (Bahloul et al., 2020).

Overall, the significance and motivation behind this research lie in its potential to address the challenges posed by big data and contribute to the development of scalable, accurate, and efficient prediction techniques (Singh, 2021). By leveraging the power of unsupervised and supervised learning, this research can unlock new possibilities for knowledge extraction, decision-making, and advancements in machine learning.

1.6 Research Gaps

Machine learning has seen tremendous growth and development over the past few years, with new techniques and algorithms being introduced constantly. However, there are still several gaps in the field of machine learning that require further research and development. This book will discuss some of the major research gaps in machine learning.

- Explain ability and Interpretability One of the major gaps in machine learning is the lack of interpretability and explain ability of models. Machine learning models are often considered as black boxes, meaning it is difficult to understand how they make predictions (Baig & Nayak, 2019). This is a significant concern, especially in critical applications such as healthcare and finance, where the decisions made by the model can have significant impacts (Fitipaldi, 2023).
- Several research efforts have been made to develop interpretable and explainable machine learning models. One approach is to use rule-based models that can be easily understood and interpreted by humans. Another approach is to develop visualization techniques that can help understand the behavior of the model. However, there is still a lot of work required to develop models that are both accurate and interpretable.
- Data Bias Another major gap in machine learning is the issue of data bias. Machine learning models are only as good as the data they are trained on. If the data used to train the model is biased, the model will also be biased. This can result in unfair and discriminatory outcomes.
- Several studies have shown that machine learning models can exhibit bias towards

certain demographics, such as race and gender. Addressing this gap requires developing methods to identify and correct for bias in the data. This can include using techniques such as data augmentation, data balancing, and adversarial training.

- Transfer Learning Transfer learning is a technique that involves transferring knowledge learned from one task to another (Fitipaldi, 2023). Transfer learning can significantly reduce the amount of data required to train a model and can improve the performance of the model. However, there are still several gaps in this area that require further research (Kumar et al., 2023).
- One major challenge in transfer learning is determining which features are transferable between tasks. This requires developing methods to identify common features across tasks and to transfer these features effectively. Another challenge is determining the optimal amount of pre-training required for transfer learning to be effective.
- Small Data and Few-Shot Learning Another gap in machine learning is the issue of small data and few-shot learning. Traditional machine learning models require a large amount of labeled data to achieve high performance. However, in many real-world applications, data is limited, and labeling data can be expensive and time-consuming (Johar, 2023).
- Few-shot learning is a technique that involves learning from only a few examples of each class. This can significantly reduce the amount of labeled data required to train a model (Kumar et al., 2023). However, there are still several gaps in this area that require further research, such as developing effective few-shot learning algorithms and determining the optimal number of examples required for few-shot learning to be effective.
- Adversarial Attacks and Robustness Adversarial attacks are a type of attack that

involves making small changes to input data to fool machine learning models. Adversarial attacks can have serious consequences, such as causing self-driving cars to misinterpret traffic signs or fooling facial recognition systems.

- Addressing this gap requires developing models that are robust to adversarial attacks. This can include using techniques such as adversarial training, which involves training the model on adversarial examples to improve robustness (Kumar et al., 2023).

- Reinforcement Learning Reinforcement learning is a technique that involves training an agent to take actions in an environment to maximize a reward. Reinforcement learning has shown promise in several applications, such as game playing and robotics. However, there are still several gaps in this area that require further research.

- One major challenge in reinforcement learning is the issue of exploration and exploitation. Reinforcement learning algorithms must balance exploration, which involves trying new actions to learn more about the environment.

1.7 Research Trends

Data Science and Machine Learning are rapidly evolving fields, which are constantly shaping and transforming the way businesses operate (Achar, 2022), and howwe approach various problems. This book will explore some of the latest research trends in data science and machine learning.

1.7.1 Deep Learning and Neural Networks:

Deep learning is a subfield of machine learning that has revolutionized the field in recent years. It is based on neural networks, which are inspired by thestructure and function of the human brain. Deep learning algorithms can automatically learn complex representations of data by iteratively processingit through multiple layers of neurons. Some of the recent research trends in deep learning include:

- **Adversarial attacks and defenses:** Adversarial attacks are techniques usedto trick deep learning models into making incorrect predictions. Recent research has focused on developing more robust deep learning models thatare resilient to adversarial attacks.
- **Explainable AI:** Deep learning models are often seen as black boxes, makingit difficult to understand how they arrived at a particular decision. ExplainableAI aims to make deep learning models more transparent, interpretable, and explainable (Gulve et al., 2023).
- **Graph Neural Networks:** Graph neural networks are a new class of deep learning models that can operate on structured data such as social networks, molecule structures, and computer networks. Recent research has shown that these models can be used to achieve state-of-the-art results on a range of tasks, including node classification, link prediction, and graph classification.

1.7.2. Reinforcement Learning:

Reinforcement learning is a type of machine learning that involves an agent learning to make decisions by trial and error in an environment. The agent receives rewards or penalties based on its actions, which are used to updateits decision-making policy (Machine Learning (ML): The Latest Trends, Developments, and Applications of ML, 2023). Recent research trends in reinforcement learninginclude:

- **Multi-Agent Reinforcement Learning:** multi-agent reinforcement learning involves multiple agents learning to collaborate or compete with each other to achieve a common goal. Recent research has shown that this approach canbe used to achieve state-of-the-art results in games such as poker and chess (Delaney et al., 2017).

- **Sample-Efficient Reinforcement Learning:** Reinforcement learning algorithms typically require a large number of samples to learn effective policies. Recent research has focused on developing algorithms that can learneffective policies with fewer samples.
- **Offline Reinforcement Learning:** Offline reinforcement learning involves learning from previously collected data, rather than interacting with the environment in real-time. Recent research has shown that this approach canbe used to learn effective policies in situations where it is difficult or expensive to collect new data.

1.7.3 Natural Language Processing:

Natural language processing (NLP) is a subfield of artificial intelligence that focuses on enabling machines to understand, interpret, and generate humanlanguage. Recent research trends in NLP include:

- **Pretrained language models:** Pretrained language models are models thatare trained on large amounts of text data and can be fine-tuned for specific NLP tasks such as sentiment analysis or text classification. Recent research has shown that these models can achieve state-of-the-art results on a rangeof NLP tasks.
- **Multilingual NLP:** Multilingual NLP involves developing models that can understand and generate multiple languages. Recent research has shown thatmultilingual models can achieve state-of-the-art results on a range of tasks and can reduce the need for language-specific models.
- **Common-Sense Reasoning:** Common-sense reasoning involves developing models that can understand and reason about the world in the same way thathumans do. Recent research has shown that incorporating common-sense knowledge into NLP models can improve their performance on a range of tasks.

1.8 Book Overview

This book is organized into several chapters, each addressing specific aspects of the research. Chapter 1 begins with an introduction to the research topic, including the background, problem statement, research objectives, and the significance of the study. Chapter 2 contains a comprehensive literature review on prediction techniques in big data, with a focus on both unsupervised and supervised learning approaches. Furthermore, technologies like HDFS, MapReduce, and YARN provide the necessary infrastructure and processing capabilities to store, process, and analyze Big Data efficiently. Chapter 3 describes the methodology employed in this research, including the research design, data collection, preprocessing techniques, and evaluation measures. Chapters 4 present the development and implementation of unsupervised and supervised learning techniques for big data prediction, respectively. Chapter 5 provides a comparative analysis and discusses the results obtained from the experiments and offers a comprehensive discussion of the findings, interpretations, limitations. Finally, Chapter 6 concludes the book by summarizing the main contributions and implications of the study and recommendations for future research (Ercan, 2015).

Through this research, it is anticipated that the proposed prediction technique will enhance the accuracy and efficiency of predictions in big data, enabling organizations to extract valuable insights and make data-driven decisions. Furthermore, this work contributes to the advancement of knowledge in the field of big data analytics and provides a foundation for future research in the domain of prediction techniques (Baig & Nayak, 2019).

Chapter 2:

Literature Review

2.1 Overview of Big Data

The world of data has undergone a significant transformation with the advent of Big Data. This term refers to the massive amounts of data generated from diverse sources such as social media platforms, the internet, sensors, and devices. This data is characterized by its enormous size and complexity, rendering traditional data processing techniques inadequate for its analysis. Consequently, Big Data analytics has emerged as a vital process for examining these vast datasets to uncover valuable insights, patterns, and correlations that can inform decision-making and enhance organizational performance. In simpler terms, the term "Big Data" refers to the data that exceeds the storage capacity and processing power of a single machine. It encompasses large volumes of data that cannot be easily managed or analyzed using traditional data processing techniques.

In the age of information, data has emerged as the lifeblood of modern enterprises, driving decisions and innovations across various industries. With the exponential growth of data, the concept of Big Data has become a pivotal element in shaping our digital landscape. This study aims to delve into the world of Big Data by identifying its critical criteria and exploring key technologies like HDFS, MapReduce, and YARN, which form the backbone of Big Data processing and storage.

2.1.1 Criteria of Big Data

To comprehend the significance of Big Data, it is essential to recognize its defining criteria, often referred to as the "5Vs": Volume, Velocity, Variety, Veracity and Value. Firstly, Volume denotes the vast amount of data generated from numerous sources, including social media, IoT devices, and sensor networks, which necessitates robust storage and processing capabilities. Secondly, Velocity signifies the speed at which data is being produced and collected in real-time, demanding efficient data handling techniques for timely analysis. Lastly, Variety encompasses the diverse types of data, including structured, semi-structured, and unstructured data, such as texts, images, videos, and more. Managing and deriving insights from this heterogeneous data is a key challenge faced by Big Data systems.

2.1.2 Understanding Hadoop Distributed File System (HDFS)

Hadoop Distributed File System (HDFS) is a fundamental component of the Apache Hadoop ecosystem, designed to store and manage vast amounts of data reliably across clusters of commodity hardware. It adheres to the principles of fault-tolerance, making it suitable for large-scale deployments. HDFS operates on a master-slave architecture, where a single NameNode oversees multiple DataNodes. The NameNode is responsible for metadata management, while DataNodes store data in blocks across the cluster. This distributed approach allows HDFS to deliver high throughput and fault tolerance, making it an ideal choice for processing Big Data workloads.

2.1.3 Understanding MapReduce

MapReduce is a programming model and processing engine that complements HDFS by enabling efficient data processing in parallel across the distributed nodes. It divides tasks into two phases: the Map phase, where data is broken down into key-value pairs and processed independently, and the Reduce phase, where the results from the Map phase are aggregated to derive meaningful insights. MapReduce inherently achieves fault tolerance, as any failed tasks can be rerun on other available nodes. However, traditional MapReduce has limitations in handling real-time data processing, which led to the emergence of other processing models like Apache Spark.

2.1.4 Master-Slave Architecture

The Master-Slave architecture is a central component in managing Big Data, but it also brings forth several critical issues and challenges. One prominent challenge is the single point of failure risk associated with the Master node. If the Master node fails, the entire system could become unavailable, leading to data processing disruptions and potential data loss. To address this concern, fault tolerance mechanisms and backup procedures must be implemented to ensure high availability and data reliability. Another issue arises from the increasing data volume and velocity, which can overwhelm the Master node's processing capabilities, resulting in performance bottlenecks. Scaling the Master-Slave architecture to handle these growing demands necessitates meticulous planning and resource allocation. Additionally, maintaining consistency between the Master and Slave nodes can become problematic in distributed environments, particularly when dealing with network partitions or node failures. Ensuring data consistency and synchronization becomes crucial to avoid data discrepancies. Lastly, the complexity of managing data distribution and load balancing among multiple Slave nodes can be challenging, requiring sophisticated load distribution algorithms and real-time monitoring. Overall, addressing these issues and challenges is vital to optimize the efficiency and effectiveness of the Master-Slave architecture in handling Big Data processing tasks.

2.1.5 Exploring Apache Hadoop YARN

Yet Another Resource Negotiator (YARN) represents the next generation of Hadoop's computational power. YARN serves as the cluster management layer in Hadoop, effectively decoupling the processing engine from the data storage, which enhances scalability and resource utilization. With YARN, multiple processing engines like MapReduce, Apache Spark, Apache Flink, and more can coexist within the same Hadoop cluster, catering to diverse application requirements. This flexibility in resource allocation and management has significantly expanded Hadoop's capabilities, making it more adaptable to varying Big Data workloads.

2.2 Big Data and Analytics

The need for Big Data and Analytics has arisen due to the exponential growth in data volume, velocity, variety, veracity and value. Data is generated incessantly from various sources, including social media platforms, sensors, devices, and more. Conventional data processing tools like spreadsheets and databases are ill-equipped to handle the magnitude and intricacy of such datasets. This is where the significance of Big Data and Analytics becomes apparent, as they enable organizations to make sense of their data and leverage it for their benefit.

Big Data analytics encompasses four main components: data collection, data storage, data processing, and data analysis. Data collection involves gathering information from diverse sources such as social media, weblogs, sensors, and other devices. Data storage entails organizing and storing this data in a manner that facilitates accessibility and swift processing. Data processing employs specialized software to process and transform the data into a format suitable for analysis. Finally, data analysis employs statistical techniques and machine learning algorithms to extract insights and discover hidden patterns within the data.

The advantages offered by Big Data and Analytics are extensive and multifaceted. One of the most significant benefits lies in the ability to make informed decisions based on data-driven insights. This empowers organizations to enhance their performance, reduce costs, and increase revenue. Big Data and Analytics also facilitate the identification of new business opportunities, the development of innovative products and services, and the improvement of the overall customer experience.

Big Data and Analytics have found applications across diverse industries, including healthcare, finance, retail, manufacturing, and more. In the healthcare sector, these technologies can be employed to enhance patient care, identify disease patterns, and predict outbreaks. The finance industry can utilize Big Data and Analytics to detect fraudulent activities, manage risks, and optimize investments. Retailers can leverage these tools to improve the customer experience, identify consumer behavior patterns, and optimize pricing strategies.

However, Big Data and Analytics present numerous challenges that organizations must address. One of the primary challenges is the sheer volume of data that necessitates processing and analysis (Avdiukhin et al., 2019). Organizations lacking the required infrastructure and expertise may find this task overwhelming. Additionally, data quality poses another challenge as Big Data is often unstructured, incomplete, and prone to errors, making it difficult to process and analyze accurately. Furthermore, privacy and security concerns are significant obstacles, given that Big Data frequently contains sensitive information that must be safeguarded.

To overcome these challenges, organizations must invest in the necessary infrastructure and expertise to handle Big Data effectively. This includes investing in high-performance computing, cloud computing, and specialized software tailored for Big Data analytics. Organizations should also establish robust data governance policies and implement stringent security measures to protect data privacy and comply with regulatory requirements.

In conclusion, Big Data and Analytics are revolutionizing the way organizations operate and make decisions. With the continuous growth in data volume, velocity, and variety, Big Data and Analytics have become indispensable. However, success in this domain necessitates investments in infrastructure, expertise, and governance policies that enable organizations to handle Big Data efficiently.

2.3 Big Data Importance

The significance of Big Data in today's business landscape cannot be overstated. It plays a crucial role in enabling organizations to thrive and remain competitive in their respective industries. Organizations that harness the power of Big Data and Analytics can gain a competitive edge and improve their performance in numerous ways. In Figure 2.1 here are some key reasons why Big Data is important:

Figure 2.1 Importance of Big Data

2.3.1 Better Decision Making: Big Data provides organizations with valuable insights that can inform decision-making processes. By leveraging Big Data analytics, organizations can analyze vast amounts of data, including customer behavior, market trends, and operational metrics. This enables them to make informed decisions based on evidence rather than relying solely on intuition or guesswork.

2.3.2 Improved Operations: Big Data analytics can uncover inefficiencies and bottlenecks within organizational processes. By analyzing large datasets, organizations can identify areas where improvements can be made, leading to cost savings, increased productivity, and streamlined operations. For example, by analyzing supply chain data, organizations can optimize inventory management and reduce wastage.

2.3.3 Enhanced Customer Experience: Big Data allows organizations to gain a deeper understanding of their customers' preferences, needs, and behaviors. By analyzing customer data, organizations can personalize their products, services, and marketing efforts to better align with customer expectations. This personalized approach leads to improved customer satisfaction, loyalty, and retention.

2.3.4 Innovation: Big Data serves as a rich source of information that can fuel innovation within organizations. By analyzing diverse datasets, organizations can identify emerging trends, market gaps, and customer demands. This information can be used to drive innovation and develop new products, services, and business models that cater to evolving market needs. Organizations that leverage Big Data for innovation gain a competitive advantage by staying ahead of the curve.

2.3.5 Risk Management: Big Data analytics plays a vital role in identifying and managing risks for organizations. By analyzing data, organizations can detect patterns and anomalies that may indicate fraudulent activities, cybersecurity threats, or compliance breaches (Fitipaldi, 2023). This proactive approach to risk management enables organizations to take appropriate measures to mitigate risks and protect their assets, reputation, and customer trust.

Big Data is of paramount importance to organizations due to its ability to facilitate better decision making, improve operations, enhance customer experience, drive innovation, and manage risks. As the volume and complexity of data continue to increase, organizations that harness the power of Big Data and leverage advanced analytics techniques will be better positioned to thrive in a rapidly evolving business landscape. Big Data has become a critical asset for organizations seeking sustainable growth, agility, and success in the digital age.

2.4 Characteristics of Big Data

Big Data is characterized by the 5Vs: Velocity, Volume, Variety, Veracity and Value. In addition to these three characteristics, there are a few more that are often associated with Big Data. In this section, will discuss the main characteristics of Big Data in detail.

Understanding and effectively managing these characteristics of Big Data is crucial for organizations to leverage its potential fully. It requires advanced technologies, such as distributed computing frameworks, scalable storage systems, real-time processing engines, machine learning algorithms, and data governance practices. Organizations that can navigate the complexities of Big Data and extract its value stand to gain significant advantages in terms of innovation, competitiveness, and performance.

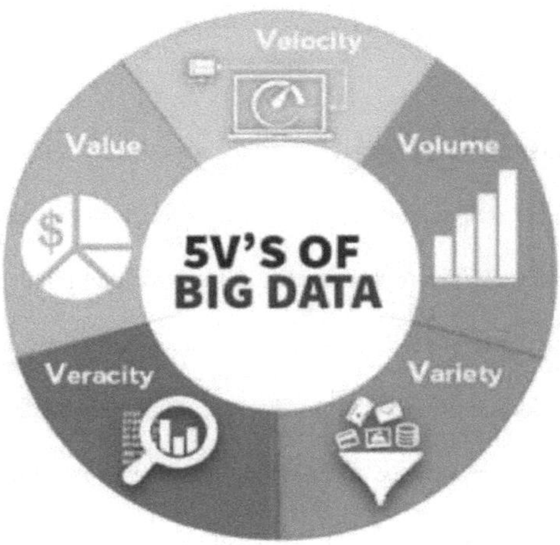

Figure 2.2 Concept Of 5V's In Big Data

In Figure 2.2 the characteristics of Big Data are essential to understanding its nature and the challenges and opportunities it presents. Let's explore each characteristic in detail:

- **Volume:** Volume refers to the vast amount of data generated and collected from various sources. It highlights the sheer scale of data that exceeds the storage and processing capabilities of traditional systems (Patel-Schneider et al, 2010). Big Data encompasses massive volumes of structured, semi-structured, and unstructured data, requiring robust infrastructure and technologies to handle and analyze.
- **Velocity:** Velocity emphasizes the speed at which data is generated, processed, and analyzed. With the advent of real-time and near real-time data sources, such as social media feeds, IoT devices, and sensor networks, organizations need to process and respond to data rapidly (Buddhakulsomsiri et al., 2006). Managing the velocity of data enables timely decision-making, insights, and actions.
- **Variety:** Variety refers to the diversity of data types and formats within Big Data. It includes structured data (e.g., relational databases), semi-structured data (e.g., XML, JSON), and unstructured data (e.g., text, images, videos). The multitude of data formats presents challenges in terms of storage, integration, and analysis, requiring flexible approaches to handle the variety effectively.
- **Veracity:** Veracity represents the quality, accuracy, and reliability of data. Big Data often contains noise, errors, inconsistencies, and biases due to data collection from numerous sources and data integration challenges. Ensuring data veracity involves data cleansing, validation, and quality control processes to ensure reliable analysis and decision-making.
- **Value:** signifies the importance of extracting meaningful insights and actionable information from Big Data (Munir et al., 2023). By analyzing and interpreting the data,

organizations can derive valuable insights that can drive business decisions, identify trends, uncover patterns, improve operational efficiency, enhance customer experiences, and gain a competitive edge. The value dimension focuses on leveraging data to create tangible and measurable outcomes.

These 5Vs collectively provide a comprehensive understanding of the characteristics and challenges associated with Big Data. Organizations must consider each dimension to effectively handle and derive value from the massive and diverse datasets available to them. By addressing the volume, velocity, variety, veracity, and value aspects of Big Data, organizations can unlock its full potential and make data-driven decisions to stay ahead in today's data-driven world.

2.5 Challenges in Big Data

While Big Data presents many opportunities for organizations, it also comes with its own set of challenges. Some of the key challenges in Big Data include:

- **Data Quality:** Big Data is often unstructured and may come from various sources, which can result in data quality issues. Poor data quality can lead to inaccurate analysis and insights, which can be detrimental to an organization.
- **Data Management:** Managing Big Data can be a challenge due to its sheer volume and variety. Organizations need to have effective data management systems in place to store, process, and analyze data efficiently.
- **Data Security:** Big Data may contain sensitive information, which makes data security a critical challenge. Organizations need to ensure that their data is secure and protected from cyber threats.
- **Data Privacy:** The use of Big Data may raise privacy concerns, especially with regulations

such as GDPR and CCPA in place. Organizations need to ensure that they comply with privacy regulations and protect the privacy of their customers and users (Asif et al., 2023).

- **Data Analysis:** Analyzing Big Data can be a challenge due to the complexity and size of the data. It requires specialized skills and tools to extract valuable insights from the data.
- **Cost:** Managing Big Data can be expensive due to the cost of infrastructure, storage, and processing. Organizations need to carefully manage their budgets to ensure that they can afford to invest in Big Data.
- **Integration:** Big Data may come from various sources and may need to be integrated with existing data sets. This can be a challenge, especially if the data is in different formats or stored in different locations.
- **Skill Gap:** Big Data requires specialized skills and knowledge, which can be a challenge for organizations that do not have the necessary expertise in-house. It can be challenging to find and retain skilled data analysts, data scientists, and other Big Data professionals.

In summary, while Big Data offers many opportunities, it also presents significant challenges. Organizations need to address these challenges to harness the power of Big Data effectively. By investing in data quality, management, security, privacy, analysis, and skills, organizations can overcome these challenges and gain valuable insights from their data.

2.6 Introduction to Technology Landscape

The technology landscape refers to the various technologies and tools that are available for organizations to use in their operations. This landscape is constantly evolving and changing, with new technologies emerging and existing technologies being updated and improved (Fitipaldi, 2023).

The technology landscape includes a wide range of technologies, such as hardware, software, networks, cloud computing, data storage, cybersecurity, artificial intelligence, machine learning, and more. These technologies can help organizations improve their efficiency, productivity, and competitiveness.

The technology landscape is constantly evolving, with new innovations and advancements emerging at a rapid pace. This dynamic environment plays a crucial role in shaping industries, businesses, and daily lives. In this section, will provide an introduction to the technology landscape, exploring its diverse aspects and the impact it has on various sectors.

- **Emerging Technologies:** The technology landscape encompasses a wide range of emerging technologies that are revolutionizing various fields. These include Artificial Intelligence (AI), Machine Learning (ML), Internet of Things (IoT), Blockchain, Virtual Reality (VR), Augmented Reality (AR), Robotics, and Quantum Computing, among others. These technologies have the potential to transform industries, disrupt traditional business models, and unlock new possibilities.
- **Digital Transformation:** The technology landscape is closely linked to the concept of digital transformation. Organizations across sectors are leveraging technology to streamline processes, enhance efficiency, and improve customer experiences. Digital transformation involves the integration of digital technologies into all aspects of an organization, fundamentally changing how they operate and deliver value (Lavanya et al, 2023).
- **Industry Impact:** The technology landscape has a profound impact on various industries, shaping their competitiveness, innovation, and growth. For example, in healthcare, advancements in medical technology, data analytics, and telemedicine are revolutionizing

patient care and treatment. In finance, technologies like Fintech, digital payments, and blockchain are transforming the way financial services are delivered. Similarly, sectors such as manufacturing, retail, transportation, and education are experiencing significant changes due to technological advancements.

- **Connectivity and Mobility:** The technology landscape is characterized by the increasing connectivity and mobility of devices and systems. The proliferation of smartphones, wearable devices, and IoT sensors has created a highly interconnected ecosystem. This connectivity enables seamless communication, data sharing, and automation, leading to improved productivity, real-time insights, and personalized experiences.
- **Data-Driven Insights:** With the vast amount of data generated and collected, the technology landscape emphasizes the importance of data-driven decision-making. Advanced analytics techniques, such as predictive analytics, data mining, and pattern recognition, enable organizations to extract valuable insights from large datasets. These insights help drive innovation, optimize processes, and identify new opportunities.
- **Cloud Computing:** Cloud computing is a fundamental component of the technology landscape. It enables organizations to access and deploy scalable computing resources, storage, and services over the internet. Cloud computing offers flexibility, cost-efficiency, and agility, allowing businesses to rapidly scale their operations and leverage advanced technologies without heavy infrastructure investments.
- **Cybersecurity:** As technology evolves, the landscape is accompanied by increased cybersecurity risks. The interconnected nature of systems and the growing number of cyber threats pose significant challenges for organizations. Cybersecurity measures, such as encryption, intrusion detection systems, and security protocols, are crucial to protect

sensitive data and maintain trust in digital environments.

- **Ethical and Social Implications:** The technology landscape raises important ethical and social considerations. As technologies like AI and automation advance, questions around job displacement, privacy, algorithmic bias, and ethical use of data arise. It is essential for organizations and policymakers to address these issues and ensure responsible and inclusive technology adoption.
- **Collaboration and Innovation:** The technology landscape fosters collaboration and innovation among industry players, researchers, and entrepreneurs. Open-source initiatives, incubators, and technology hubs provide platforms for collaboration and knowledge exchange. These collaborations drive the development of new technologies, applications, and business models.
- **Continuous Evolution:** The technology landscape is in a constant state of evolution. New technologies emerge, existing ones evolve, and trends shift over time. Staying updated with the latest developments, conducting research, and embracing a culture of continuous learning are essential to navigate the technology landscape effectively. In today's rapidly changing business environment, organizations need to keep up with the latest technologies to remain competitive. They need to invest in technology infrastructure, tools, and resources to leverage the power of technology effectively. This requires careful planning and strategic decision-making, as well as the ability to adapt to new technologies quickly.

The technology landscape also presents challenges and risks, such as security threats, data breaches, and privacy concerns. Organizations need to be aware of these risks and take measures to mitigate them. They need to implement cybersecurity measures, adhere to data privacy regulations, and stay up to date on the latest security threats and vulnerabilities (Munir et al., 2023).

The technology landscape is a critical aspect of modern business operations. Organizations need to stay up to date on the latest technologies and tools and invest in them strategically to stay competitive (Nanni et al., 2020). They also need to address the risks and challenges associated with technology to ensure that they can leverage its power effectively and safely.

In conclusion, the technology landscape is a dynamic and multifaceted environment that shapes industries, organizations, and society as a whole. Its impact extends across sectors, enabling digital transformation, driving innovation, and presenting both challenges and opportunities. Understanding and harnessing the potential of the technology landscape are crucial for organizations to thrive in today's rapidly changing world.

2.7 Overview of Data Science and Machine Learning

Data science and machine learning are two fields that have experienced tremendous growth and development in recent years. Both fields are focused on extracting insights and knowledge from data, but they use different techniques and approaches to achieve this goal (Achar, 2022).

2.7.1 Data Science: Data science is an interdisciplinary field that involves the use of scientific methods, processes, algorithms, and systems to extract insights and knowledge from structured and unstructured data. It includes various subfields such as data mining, data analysis, machine learning, and statistics (Delaney et al., 2017). The goal of data science is to extract valuable insights from data that can help organizations make better decisions.

The Cyclic Process of Data Science is a structured methodology that outlines the iterative steps involved in extracting valuable insights and knowledge from data. In Figure 2.3 the cyclic process of data science emphasizes the iterative nature of data science, where each completed cycle enhances the accuracy and understanding of the data, driving ongoing improvements and discoveries.

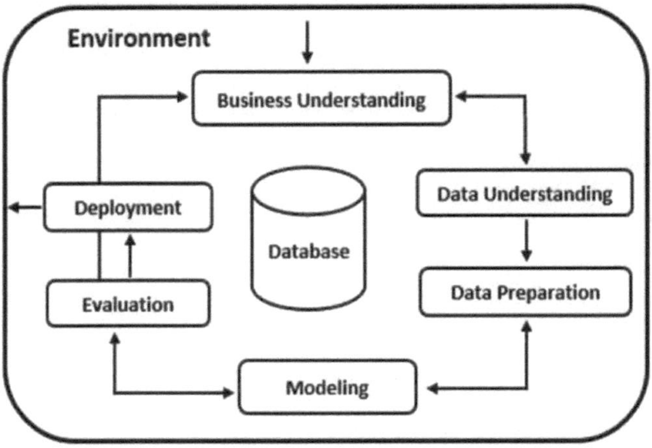

Figure 2.3 Cyclic Process of Data Science

The data science process involves several steps:

- **Business Understanding:** The first step is to identify the problem you want to solve and clearly define objectives.
- **Understanding/Collecting Data:** The second step is to collect data from various sources. This may involve using data scraping tools, surveying customers, or analyzing existing data sets.
- **Preprocessing/Cleaning Data:** The third step is to clean and process the data. This may involve removing missing values, transforming data, and normalizing data. This step is also to perform exploratory data analysis to understand the patterns and relationships in the data (Munir et al., 2023).
- **Model Building:** The fourth step is to build a model using machine learning algorithms

to predict outcomes or detect patterns. This is process which producing a descriptive diagram of relationships between various type of information.

- **Evaluation And Validation:** The fifth step is to evaluate the model's performance and validate its accuracy using metrics such as confusion matrix, precision, recall, and F1 score (Singh, 2021).
- **Deployment:** The sixth and final step is to deploy the model in a production environment and monitor its performance regularly.

2.7.2 Machine Learning: Machine learning is a subfield of artificial intelligence that involves building algorithms that can learn from data and make predictions or decisions without being explicitly programmed. Machine learning algorithms are designed to improve their performance over time as they are exposed to more data (Ahmed et al., 2020).

Three Main Types of Machine Learning Approaches:

Supervised Learning: In supervised learning, the algorithm is trained on labeled data, meaning that the data includes both input features and the correct output. The algorithm learns to map the input features to the correct output, and then can predict the output for new, unseen data (Mustafakulov & Arzikulov, 2020). In Figure 2.4 there is an agent in supervised learning environment, which process the given input and gets the output. But teacher has desired output or answer to verify it. Commonly used techniques are Regression, Classification etc.

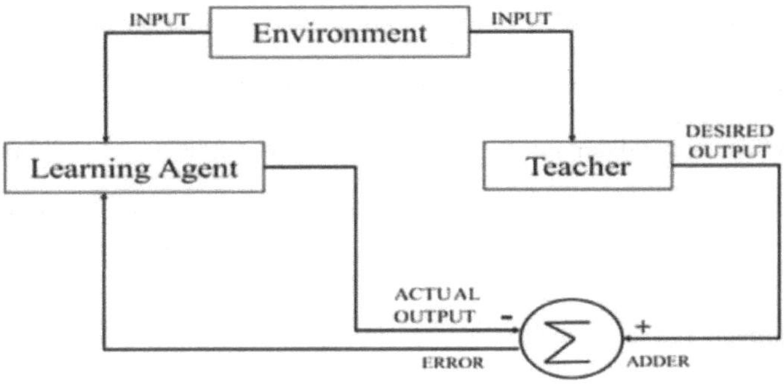

Figure 2.4 Supervised Learning

- **Unsupervised Learning:** In unsupervised learning, the algorithm is trained on unlabeled data, meaning that there is no correct output. The algorithm learns to identify patterns and relationships in the data and can group similar data points together.

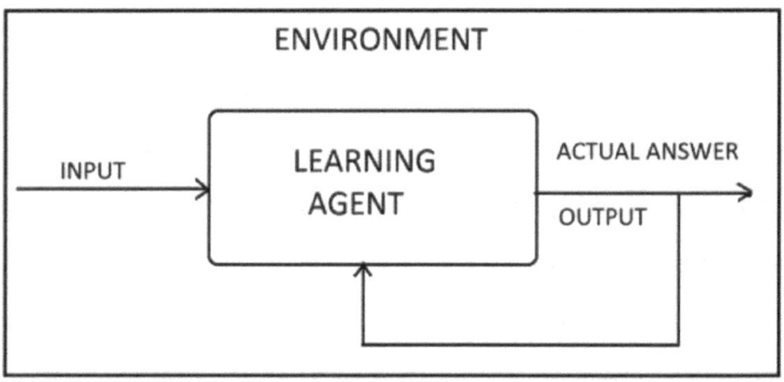

Figure 2.5 Unsupervised Learning

In Figure 2.5 Unsupervised Learning does not have any teacher. The learning agent does not know current answer. Learning agent takes input from surrounding environment. Unsupervised Learning agent efforts to learn itself from the patterns with no corresponding output values. Commonly used techniques are Clustering, Association Rule, Sequential Pattern etc.

- **Reinforcement Learning:** In reinforcement learning, the algorithm learns by interacting with an environment and receiving feedback in the form of rewards or punishments. The algorithm learns to maximize its rewards by taking actions that lead to positive outcomes. Machine learning algorithms can be used for a wide range of applications, including image recognition, speech recognition, natural language processing, fraud detection, and recommendation systems (Delaney et al., 2017).

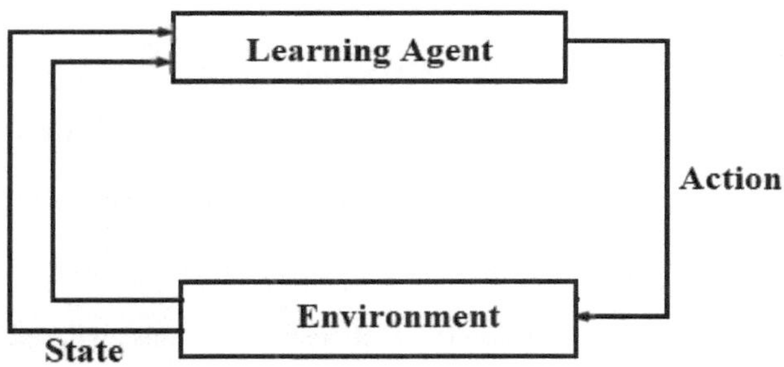

Figure 2.6 Reinforcement Learning

In Figure 2.6 the entity that performs the configuration can be either the driver itself (agent) or a track engineer (supervisor). With the phrase environment configuration, it is being refer to the activity of altering some environmental parameters to improve the performance of the agent's policy. Commonly used techniques are Queue Learning, Reward Matrix, Maximization etc.

2.7.3 Data Science vs. Machine Learning:

Data science and machine learning are closely related but have some important differences. Data science is a broader field that encompasses many different techniques for working with data, including data analysis, data visualization, and data mining (Achar, 2022). Machine learning is a specific type of data science that involves building models that can learn from data and make predictions. While data science focuses on understanding and interpreting data, machine learning focuses on building predictive models. Data science is more exploratory in nature, while machine learning is more goal-oriented.

Data science and machine learning both require a strong foundation in mathematics and statistics, as well as programming skills. Data scientists must be proficient in languages such as Python, R, and SQL, while machine learning engineers may also need to be proficient in languages such as Java or C++.

2.8 Prediction Techniques in Machine Learning

Machine learning has revolutionized the field of data analysis and prediction. With the ability to automatically learn patterns and make predictions from data, machine learning techniques have found applications in various domains, including finance, healthcare, marketing, and more. In this review, will explore the landscape of prediction techniques in machine learning, discussing their strengths, weaknesses, and real-world applications (Singh, 2021).

Machine learning prediction techniques have revolutionized various industries by enabling accurate predictions and insights from large and complex datasets. In this review, will explore different machine learning prediction techniques and their applications, highlighting their strengths, limitations, and recent advancements.

2.8.1 Supervised Learning Techniques:

Supervised learning is a widely used prediction technique where a model learns patterns and relationships between input variables (features) and corresponding output variables (labels) from labeled training data (Mustafakulov & Arzikulov, 2020). The model then predicts the labels for new, unseen data. Common algorithms used in supervised learning include linear regression, logistic regression, decision trees, random forests, support vector machines, and neural networks (Avdiukhin et al., 2019).

Supervise Learning techniques rely on the set of past transactions for which the label (also referred to as outcome or class) of the transaction is known. It is technique in which teacher or trainer, teach or train the machine using data, which is well label.

- Learning agent and trainer both takes input from surrounding environment but the trainer has desired output or result.
- There is a learning agent, which process the given input and gets the output.
- The actual output subtracted from the desired output by the adder, which shows the error in a output.
- The error injected as input to learning agent so that it can learn from the error while generatin output from the next time and can remove the error.
- Data are label and may already know the output with the help of trainer.
- Techniques of Supervised learning are-Regression, Classification and Deviation Detection.
- Algorithms of Supervised Learning are-
- Regression, Decision tree, Random Forest, SVM and Naïve-Bayes.
- Table 2.1 explains the Strengths & Limitations of Supervised Learning Techniques.

Table 2.1 Supervised Learning Techniques Strengths & Limitations.

Strengths	Limitations
Well-established and extensively studied technique with a strong theoretical foundation.	Requires labeled training data, which can be expensive and time-consuming to acquire.
Effective for tasks such as classification, regression, and time series forecasting.	May struggle with overfitting if the model is too complex or the dataset is small.
Can handle complex relationships between variables and capture nonlinear patterns.	Limited interpretability for certain algorithms like neural networks.
Performs well when training data is abundant and representative.	Performance may degrade when applied to new data that differs significantly from the training set.

Recent Advancements:

- **Deep Learning:** Deep neural networks with multiple hidden layers have achieved remarkable success in various domains, including image recognition, natural language processing, and speech recognition.
- **Transfer Learning:** This approach allows models trained on one task to be used as a starting point for solving related tasks, reducing the need for extensive labeled data.
- **Ensemble Methods:** Combining multiple models (e.g., bagging, boosting, stacking) can improve prediction accuracy and robustness.

2.8.2 Unsupervised Learning Techniques:

Unsupervised learning aims to identify patterns and structures in unlabeled data without explicit guidance. It is particularly useful for exploratory data analysis, clustering, and anomaly detection. It is a process of training machine using information unlabeled and allowing the algorithm to act on that information without guidance. It does not have any trainer, which means that correct answer is unknown to the learning agent. UL is becoming more and more popular because it does not need manually annotated data, especially in the current rapid growth of data.

- Unsupervised Learning does not have any teacher.
- The learning agent does not know actual output.
- In Unsupervised Learning agent have to learn itself from the patterns and meaningful correlations wit the corresponding output.
- Information clusters based on feature similarities.
- Techniques used in unsupervised learning are-Clustering, Association Rule Mining and Sequen Pattern.

- Algorithms of Unsupervised Learning are-
- K-Means, Market Basket Analysis, Apriori Algorithm
- Table 2.2 explains the Strengths & Limitations of Unsupervised Learning Techniques.

Table 2.2 Unsupervised Learning Techniques Strengths & Limitations.

Strengths	Limitations
Does not require labeled data, making it suitable for scenarios where labeling is difficult or unavailable.	Lack of explicit ground truth makes evaluation challenging.
Can reveal hidden structures and relationships within data.	Subjective interpretation of results requires domain expertise.
Helps in identifying outliers, anomalies, and discovering unknown patterns.	Performance heavily relies on data quality and preprocessing.
Enables data visualization and summarization.	Scalability can be an issue when dealing with large datasets.

Recent Advancements:

- **Deep Generative Models:** Variational autoencoders (VAEs) and generative adversarial networks (GANs) have enabled the synbook of realistic and high-dimensional data samples.
- **Representation Learning:** Unsupervised learning can be used as a pretraining step to learn useful representations that can benefit downstream tasks like supervised learning.
- **Anomaly Detection:** Novel techniques, such as one-class SVMs, deep autoencoders, and Isolation Forests, have improved anomaly detection accuracy and scalability.

2.8.3 Reinforcement Learning Techniques:

Reinforcement learning involves an agent interacting with an environment to learn optimal decision-making policies through trial and error. The agent receives feedback in the form of rewards or penalties based on its actions, allowing it to optimize its behavior over time. Reinforcement learning has gained significant attention in areas such as robotics, game playing, and autonomous systems (Gulve et al., 2023).

Reinforcement learning is a part from advances Machine Learning where an agent placed in an environment and it learns to behave in this environment by performing positive actions through observation and get the rewards, which it gets from those actions.

- It is the part of advances Machine Learning.
- The technique used in Reinforcement Learning is totally reward based.
- It learns from the environment.
- It takes the data from the environment and analyses it.
- Algorithms of Reinforcement Learning are- Queue Learning, Reward Matrix, Maximization, Macron Decision Process.
- Table 2.3 explains the Strengths & Limitations of Reinforcement Learning Techniques.

Table 2.3 Reinforcement Learning Techniques Strengths & Limitations.

Strengths	Limitations
Well-suited for sequential decision-making problems.	High sample complexity and computational requirements.
Can learn in dynamic and changing environments.	Learning from scratch can be time-consuming.
Enables the agent to learn optimal strategies without explicit instructions.	Lack of interpretability and transparency in decision-making.

Each technique has its strengths, weaknesses, and real-world applications. Linear regression is suitable for simple linear relationships, while decision trees and random forests offer interpretability and handle both categorical and numerical data. Support vector machines provide effective classification with complex decision boundaries, while neural networks and deep learning excel in learning intricate patterns. Gradient boosting combines weak models for powerful predictions, and time series forecasting techniques cater specifically to sequential data. Bayesian networks handle uncertain data and allow for probabilistic inference.

Choosing the right prediction technique depends on the nature of the problem, the available data, computational resources, and interpretability requirements (Buggenthin et al., 2017). Often, a combination of techniques and ensemble methods can yield superior results. As machine learning continues to advance, new prediction techniques are emerging, providing exciting opportunities for predictive analytics in various domains.

2.9 Critical Analysis of Existing Literature

Big data, data science, and machine learning have gained significant attention in recent years due to their potential to unlock valuable insights and drive innovation across various domains. As a result, a vast body of literature has emerged, providing insights, methodologies, and frameworks in these fields. In this critical analysis, will examine the existing literature on big data, data science, and machine learning, evaluating its strengths, limitations, and potential areas for future research.

2.9.1 Big Data Literature:

The literature on big data encompasses a wide range of topics, including data acquisition, storage, processing, analysis, and visualization. Many studies highlight the transformative impact of big data on decision-making, innovation, and business performance. However, a common limitation is the lack of focus on the ethical, legal, and societal implications of big data. Future research should address these issues to ensure responsible and ethical use of data.

2.9.2 Data Science Literature:

Data science literature explores the interdisciplinary nature of extracting knowledge and insights from data through statistical and computational techniques. It covers topics such as data preprocessing, feature selection, modeling, and evaluation (Munoz-Rodriguez et al., 1992). The literature emphasizes the importance of understanding the context and domain knowledge when applying data science methods (Levine et al., 2008). However, there is a need for more research on interpretability, fairness, and transparency of data science models, as these aspects are crucial for building trust and accountability.

2.9.3 Machine Learning Literature:

Machine learning literature encompasses a wide range of algorithms and techniques for pattern recognition, classification, regression, and clustering. Many studies demonstrate the effectiveness of machine learning in various applications, including healthcare, finance, and marketing. However, there is a common challenge of generalizability, as models trained on specific datasets may not perform well in different contexts. Addressing this challenge requires more research on transfer learning, domain adaptation, and robustness of machine learning models.

2.9.4 Integration of Big Data, Data Science and Machine Learning:

The integration of big data, data science, and machine learning is a rapidly evolving area of research. Studies highlight the potential of combining these disciplines to harness the power of data and drive innovation. However, there is a need for more comprehensive frameworks and methodologies that address the challenges of scalability, interpretability, and ethical considerations in complex data-driven systems.

2.9.5 Limitations and Future Directions:

While the existing literature provides valuable insights, there are several limitations that need to be addressed. First, there is a lack of standardized benchmarks and evaluation metrics, making it difficult to compare and replicate research findings. Second, there is a need for more research on real-time and streaming analytics, as traditional batch processing may not be sufficient for handling dynamic big data streams. Third, the literature often lacks consideration of contextual factors and the human element in data analysis, which can significantly impact the effectiveness and usability of data-driven solutions.

Future research should focus on addressing these limitations and exploring emerging topics such as explainable AI, fairness, privacy-preserving techniques, and ethical frameworks for big data, data science, and machine learning. Interdisciplinary collaborations and partnerships between academia, industry, and policymakers are essential to drive impactful research and ensure the responsible and beneficial use of data-driven technologies (Amirian et al, 2017).

The existing literature on big data, data science, and machine learning provides valuable insights and methodologies for unlocking the potential of data-driven decision-making and innovation. However, it is essential to address the limitations and challenges to advance the field further. Future research should focus on interdisciplinary approaches, ethical considerations, interpretability, scalability, and real-time analytics to fully realize the transformative power of big data, data science, and machine learning in various domains. By addressing these research gaps, can pave the way for responsible and effective data-driven solutions that contribute to societal, economic, and technological advancements.

2.10 Summary of Gaps in Literature

Big data, data science, and machine learning have emerged as critical fields in the era of data-driven decision-making and innovation. However, despite the vast amount of literature available on these subjects, there are still significant gaps and areas for further research and exploration. In this summary, will highlight some of the key gaps in the existing literature on big data, data science, and machine learning, and discuss the importance of addressing these gaps for advancing the field.

2.10.1 Ethical Considerations:

One major gap in the literature is the limited focus on ethical considerations in the collection, storage, processing, and analysis of big data. As the amount of data being generated and analyzed increases, it is crucial to address issues such as privacy, security, bias, fairness, and transparency (Arcadius Tokognon et al., 2017). Future research should explore ethical frameworks and guidelines for big data, data science, and machine learning to ensure responsible and accountable use of data-driven technologies.

2.10.2 Interdisciplinary Approaches:

While big data, data science, and machine learning are inherently interdisciplinary fields, there is still a need for more research that bridges the gaps between various disciplines. Collaborations between computer science, statistics, mathematics, social sciences, and domain-specific fields are essential to develop comprehensive solutions and methodologies.

Interdisciplinary approaches can help in addressing complex challenges and leveraging the full potential of data-driven technologies.

2.10.3 Interpretability and Explainability:

The lack of interpretability and explainability in machine learning models is another significant gap in the literature. As machine learning algorithms become more complex, it becomes increasingly challenging to understand and interpret their decision-making processes. This gap hinders trust, accountability, and adoption of machine learning in critical domains such as healthcare and finance. Future research should focus on developing interpretable and explainable machine learning models to enhance transparency and enable human understanding of the underlying processes.

2.10.4 Scalability and Real-Time Analytics:

The scalability of big data processing and real-time analytics are areas that require further exploration. Traditional data processing techniques may not be sufficient to handle the massive volume and velocity of data being generated. Future research should focus on developing scalable algorithms, frameworks, and architectures that can efficiently process and analyze big data in real-time. This includes exploring distributed computing, streaming analytics, and edge computing approaches to handle the increasing demands of data processing.

2.10.5 Data Quality and Preprocessing:

Another critical gap in the literature is the limited emphasis on data quality and preprocessing. Big data often consists of noisy, incomplete, and unstructured data, which can affect the accuracy and reliability of analysis results. Future research should focus on developing effective data cleansing, preprocessing, and feature selection techniques to improve the quality of big data and enhance the performance of data-driven models.

2.10.5 Contextual Factors and Human-Centric Approaches:

The literature often overlooks the importance of contextual factors and human-centric approaches in data analysis. Understanding the context in which data is collected and the needs of end-users is crucial for the successful implementation of data-driven solutions. Future research should explore the integration of contextual information, domain knowledge, and human feedback into the data analysis process. This will enable the development of more effective and user-centered data-driven systems.

In conclusion, while the literature on big data, data science, and machine learning provides valuable insights and methodologies, there are significant gaps that need to be addressed for the field to advance further. Ethical considerations, interdisciplinary approaches, interpretability, scalability, data quality, and human-centric approaches are among the key areas requiring attention. By addressing these gaps through rigorous research and collaboration, this can pave the way for responsible, transparent, and impactful data-driven solutions that contribute to societal, economic, and technological advancements.

Finally, the chapter concludes with a summary of the gaps identified in the literature. These gaps represent areas where further research is needed or where the current understanding is limited. Identifying these gaps gives a rationale for the research study and highlights its potential contribution to the field.

Chapter 3:

Methodology and Proposed Framework

3.1 Research Design and Approach

The development of effective prediction techniques in the context of big data has become crucial in various domains, such as finance, healthcare, and marketing. This chapter presents the research design and approach that will be employed to develop a prediction technique using both unsupervised and supervised learning perspectives (Simon et al, 2003). The research design outlines the overall structure and methodology of the study, while the research approach describes the specific techniques and tools that will be utilized.

3.1.1 Research Design

The research design for this study follows a systematic and structured approach, consisting of several key steps:

i. **Problem Identification:** The first step involves identifying the specific problem or prediction task that will be addressed. This may include tasks such as customer churn prediction, fraud detection, or sentiment analysis.

ii. **Data Collection:** The second step is to gather relevant data for the prediction task. This may involve collecting large volumes of structured or unstructured data from various sources, such as databases, social media platforms, or sensor networks (Wiggins, 2023).

iii. **Data Preprocessing:** Once the data is collected, it needs to be preprocessed to ensure its quality and suitability for analysis. This step includes data cleaning, handling missing values, normalization, and feature extraction (Staszak et al., 2023).

iv. **Unsupervised Learning:** The next step is to apply unsupervised learning techniques to explore the data and identify patterns or clusters within it (Nanni et al., 2020). This may involve employing clustering algorithms such as k-means, hierarchical clustering, or DBSCAN to group similar data points together (Avdiukhin et al., 2019).

v. **Feature Extraction and Dimensionality Reduction:** In this step, relevant features are extracted from the data and dimensionality reduction techniques such as principal component analysis (PCA) or t-SNE (t-Distributed Stochastic Neighbor Embedding) are applied to reduce the dimensionality of the dataset while preserving important information (Jha, 2015).

vi. **Supervised Learning:** After the unsupervised learning phase, the dataset is labeled based on the identified patterns or clusters. Supervised learning algorithms are then employed to build prediction models. This may include classification algorithms like decision trees, random forests, or support vector machines, as well as regression algorithms like linear regression or neural networks.

vii. **Model Evaluation:** The performance of the prediction models is assessed using suitable evaluation metrics, such as accuracy, precision, recall, or mean squared error. Cross-validation techniques may be employed to ensure robustness and generalizability of the models (Baig & Nayak, 2019).

viii. **Comparison and Analysis:** The results obtained from unsupervised and supervised learning approaches are compared and analyzed to determine their effectiveness and suitability for the given prediction task. This analysis may involve examining the predictive accuracy, computational efficiency, interpretability, and scalability of the developed techniques.

3.1.2 Research Approach

The research approach for this study will involve the following techniques and tools:

I. **Programming Languages:** The prediction technique will be developed using popular programming languages such as Python, which provide extensive libraries and frameworks for data analysis and machine learning (Singh, 2020).

II. **Data Mining and Machine Learning Libraries:** Various data mining and machine learning libraries, such as scikit-learn, TensorFlow, or PyTorch, will be utilized for implementing the unsupervised and supervised learning algorithms, as well as for data preprocessing and model evaluation.

III. **Experimental Setup:** The experiments will be conducted on a suitable computing environment, such as a high-performance computing cluster or cloud-based infrastructure, to handle the large volumes of big data and ensure efficient processing (Sangaiah, 2019).

IV. **Evaluation Metrics:** Standard evaluation metrics specific to the prediction task will be employed to assess the performance of the developed technique. These metrics may include accuracy, precision, recall, F1-score, or area under the receiver operating characteristic (ROC) curve (Singh, 2021).

V. **Comparative Analysis:** A comprehensive comparative analysis will be conducted to evaluate the strengths and weaknesses of the unsupervised and supervised learning approaches. This analysis will help in understanding the trade (Sangaiah, 2019).

3.2 Data Collection and Pre-Processing

Data collection and pre-processing are fundamental steps in developing a prediction technique using unsupervised and supervised learning approaches (Ledziński & Grześk, 2023). This section discusses the process of data collection, the importance of quality data, and the pre-processing steps required to ensure the suitability of the data for analysis.

3.2.1 Data Collection

The success of any prediction technique heavily relies on the quality and relevance of the data used. In the context of big data, the volume, velocity, variety, and veracity of data pose significant challenges (Ercan, 2015). Therefore, a well-designed data collection strategy is essential. The following steps should be considered during data collection:

i. **Define the Objective:** Clearly define the prediction task and the specific data requirements. Determine the variables, features, and target variables that are necessary for the analysis.

ii. **Identify Data Sources:** Identify relevant data sources that can provide the required information. These sources can include databases, data warehouses, APIs, social media platforms, sensor networks, or third-party data providers.

iii. **Data Gathering:** Collect the data from the identified sources using appropriate methods. This can involve web scraping, data extraction, data mining techniques, or direct data integration from various sources.

iv. **Data Storage and Management:** Establish a data storage and management system that ensures data integrity, security, and easy access for analysis. This can involve using databases, data lakes, or cloud storage solutions.

3.2.2 Data Pre-Processing

Data pre-processing is a crucial step that prepares the collected data for analysis. It involves several techniques to clean, transform, and enhance the data quality. The following pre-processing steps are commonly performed:

i. **Data Cleaning:** Identify and handle missing values, outliers, duplicate records, and inconsistent data. This can involve imputing missing values, removing or correcting outliers, and resolving inconsistencies.

ii. **Data Integration:** Integrate data from multiple sources into a unified dataset. This involves resolving differences in data formats, units, and structures.

iii. **Data Transformation:** Transform the data to meet the requirements of the prediction technique and improve its quality. Common transformations include normalization, standardization, logarithmic transformation, or scaling.

iv. **Feature Selection:** Select relevant features that have a significant impact on the prediction task. This can involve techniques such as correlation analysis, feature importance ranking, or domain knowledge-based selection.

v. **Feature Engineering:** Create new features or derive meaningful representations from the existing features. This can include techniques such as feature extraction, polynomial features, binning, or one-hot encoding.

vi. **Dimensionality Reduction:** Reduce the dimensionality of the dataset to alleviate the curse of dimensionality and improve computational efficiency. Techniques such as principal component analysis (PCA), linear discriminant analysis (LDA), or t-SNE can be used.

vii. **Data Sampling:** Address class imbalance or data skewness issues through sampling techniques such as oversampling, under sampling, or synthetic data generation.

viii. **Data Splitting:** Split the pre-processed data into training, validation, and test sets. The training set is used to build the prediction models, the validation set is used for model tuning, and the test set is used for final evaluation.

By performing these pre-processing steps, the collected data is transformed into a suitable format for analysis using unsupervised and supervised learning techniques. Data quality is enhanced, irrelevant information is removed, and the data is prepared to extract meaningful patterns and relationships. Data collection and pre-processing play a crucial role in the development of a prediction technique using unsupervised and supervised learning. By carefully collecting relevant data and applying appropriate pre-processing techniques, the data becomes suitable for analysis and increases the likelihood of accurate and reliable predictions.

3.3 Unsupervised Learning in Big Data Prediction

Unsupervised learning techniques and algorithms play a crucial role in developing prediction techniques by extracting valuable insights and patterns from unlabeled data. In this section, will explore various unsupervised learning techniques and algorithms that can be employed in the development of a prediction technique using both unsupervised and supervised learning approaches (Levine et al., 2008).

3.3.1 Clustering Techniques:

Clustering techniques are widely used in unsupervised learning to group similar data points together based on their inherent characteristics. Clustering helps in identifying natural groupings within the data, which can be valuable for segmentation, anomaly detection, and exploratory analysis. Let's discuss some commonly utilized clustering techniques:

i. **K-means Clustering:** K-means is a popular clustering algorithm that aims to partition the data into K clusters, where K is a user-defined parameter. It minimizes the within-cluster sum of squares by iteratively assigning data points to clusters and updating the cluster centroids (Principato et al., 2023).

ii. **Hierarchical Clustering:** Hierarchical clustering builds a hierarchy of clusters, creating a tree-like structure known as a dendrogram. It can be agglomerative (bottom-up) or divisive (top-down), merging or splitting clusters based on their similarity.

iii. **DBSCAN (Density-Based Spatial Clustering of Applications with Noise):** DBSCAN is a density-based clustering algorithm that groups data points based on their density. It identifies dense regions and separates outliers as noise, making it suitable for complex cluster shapes.

iv. **Gaussian Mixture Models (GMM):** GMM assumes that the data points are generated from a mixture of Gaussian distributions. It estimates the parameters of these distributions to identify the underlying clusters. Clustering techniques enable the discovery of hidden structures and patterns in the data, providing valuable insights for subsequent analysis and prediction (Supervised Vs Unsupervised Machine Learning, 2023).

3.3.2 Dimensionality Reduction Techniques:

Dimensionality reduction techniques are employed to reduce the number of features or variables in the dataset while preserving essential information. These techniques help mitigate the curse of dimensionality, improve computational efficiency, and aid in visualizing high-dimensional data. Let's explore some commonly used dimensionality reduction techniques:

i. **Principal Component Analysis (PCA):** PCA is a linear dimensionality reduction technique that transforms the original features into a new set of orthogonal features called principal components. These components capture the maximum variance in the data, allowing for dimensionality reduction.

ii. **t-SNE (t-Distributed Stochastic Neighbor Embedding):** t-SNE is a nonlinear dimensionality reduction technique that maps high-dimensional data to a low-dimensional space while preserving the local structure and clustering relationships. It is particularly useful for visualizing complex patterns in two or three dimensions (Lalla-Ruiz et al, 2020).

iii. **Autoencoders:** Autoencoders are neural networks that learn to reconstruct the input data from a compressed representation called the bottleneck layer. By training the autoencoder to minimize the reconstruction error, it learns a lower-dimensional representation of the data (Jemili & Korbaa, 2023).

iv. Dimensionality reduction techniques help in feature selection, noise reduction, and capturing the most relevant information for prediction tasks.

3.3.3. Association Rule Mining:

Association rule mining is a technique used to discover interesting relationships or associations among items in a dataset. It is particularly useful in market basket analysis and recommendation systems. The most well-known algorithm for association rule mining is the Apriori algorithm, which identifies frequent item sets and generates association rules based on user-defined thresholds.

Association rule mining helps in understanding the dependencies and co-occurrences among items, enabling predictions and recommendations based on these associations.

3.3.4. Anomaly Detection Techniques:

Anomaly detection techniques focus on identifying unusual or anomalous instances in the data, which can be indicative of potential fraud, errors, or outliers. Anomalies often deviate significantly from the norm and require special attention. Some commonly employed anomaly detection techniques include:

i. **Density-Based Anomaly Detection:** These techniques identify anomalies as data points that lie in regions of significantly low density compared to the majority of the data. DBSCAN, mentioned earlier as a clustering algorithm, can also be used for density-based anomaly detection.

ii. **Distance-Based Anomaly Detection:** These techniques identify anomalies based on the distance or dissimilarity of data points from their neighbors. The Local Outlier Factor (LOF) algorithm computes the local density of a data point relative to its neighbors to identify anomalies.

ii. **Isolation Forest:** The Isolation Forest algorithm isolates anomalies by constructing isolation trees. Anomalies are easier to isolate and require fewer splits to separate from normal data points.

Anomaly detection techniques help in identifying and flagging unusual instances that may impact the accuracy and reliability of predictions.

The unsupervised learning techniques and algorithms, including clustering, dimensionality reduction, association rule mining, and anomaly detection, are instrumental in developing prediction techniques using unsupervised and supervised learning approaches (Mathai et al, 2023). These techniques enable the discovery of patterns, reduction of data dimensionality, identification of associations, and detection of anomalies, ultimately enhancing the accuracy and effectiveness of prediction models.

3.4 Supervised Learning in Big Data Prediction

Supervised learning is a powerful approach in big data prediction that leverages labeled data to train predictive models. With the abundance of data generated in various domains, such as healthcare, finance, and e-commerce, supervised learning techniques offer valuable insights and enable accurate predictions. This book will explore the significance of supervised learning in big data prediction and discuss various techniques used in this context (Delaney et al., 2017). Supervised learning algorithms learn from labeled examples to make predictions or classify new, unseen data. They require a training dataset consisting of input features and corresponding target labels (Bhushan & Agarwal,2023). The goal is to build a model that can generalize from the training data and make accurate predictions on unseen data. Let's delve into some key supervised learning techniques and their applications in big data prediction:

3.4.1. Decision Trees:

Decision trees are widely used in supervised learning due to their interpretability and ability to handle both categorical and numerical data (Ayodele, 2010). These models partition the data based on feature values and create a tree-like structure to make predictions. Decision tree algorithms, such as C4.5 and CART, recursively split the data based on the most informative features, enabling accurate predictions (Jha, 2015).

- Credit risk assessment: Decision trees can be used to predict the likelihood of loan default based on customer attributes, enabling banks to make informed lending decisions.
- Disease diagnosis: Decision trees help in diagnosing diseases based on patient symptoms, aiding in early detection and treatment.

3.4.2. Random Forests:

Random forests are an ensemble learning technique that combines multiple decision trees to make predictions. Each tree is trained on a random subset of the data and features, reducing overfitting and improving generalization. By aggregating the predictions of individual trees, random forests provide robust and accurate predictions (Orero Blat, 2023).

- Customer churn prediction: Random forests can be used to predict customer churn based on historical customer data, enabling businesses to take proactive retention measures.
- Image classification: Random forests are effective in classifying images based on their visual features, making them valuable in various computer vision tasks.

3.4.3. Support Vector Machines (SVM):

Support Vector Machines are powerful supervised learning algorithms used for classification and regression tasks. SVMs find a hyperplane that maximally separates data points of different classes or predicts continuous values. They are effective in handling high-dimensional data and can handle both linear and non-linear relationships (Buggenthin et al., 2017).

- Spam detection: SVMs can classify emails as spam or non-spam based on textual features, helping in filtering unwanted emails.
- Stock market prediction: SVMs can be used to predict stock prices based on historical market data, assisting investors in making informed trading decisions (Abramowicz & Kokkinaki, 2014).

3.4.4. Neural Networks:

Neural networks, particularly deep learning models, have gained significant popularity in big data prediction. They consist of multiple interconnected layers of artificial neurons that learn complex representations from the data. Deep learning models, such as convolutional neural networks (CNNs) and recurrent neural networks (RNNs), have achieved remarkable performance in various domains.

- Image recognition: CNNs excel in tasks like object detection and image classification, enabling applications like autonomous driving and facial recognition.
- Natural language processing: RNNs are effective in language modeling, machine translation, and sentiment analysis, making them valuable in analyzing textual data.

3.4.5. Gradient Boosting:

Gradient boosting is an ensemble learning technique that combines weak predictive models, typically decision trees, to create a strong predictive model. It iteratively trains new models to correct the errors of previous models, gradually improving prediction accuracy.

- Click-through rate prediction: Gradient boosting models can predict the probability of a user clicking on an online advertisement, enabling targeted ad placements.
- Customer lifetime value prediction: Gradient boosting can estimate the future value of a customer, aiding in customer segmentation and personalized marketing strategies.

The supervised learning techniques offer valuable tools for prediction in big data scenarios. Decision trees, random forests, support vector machines, neural networks, and gradient boosting are among the prominent algorithms used in this domain (Gasteiger, 2003). These techniques enable accurate predictions, classification, and regression tasks across various industries, contributing to improved decision-making, personalized recommendations, and optimized operations. As big data continues to grow, the application of supervised learning in prediction tasks will play a crucial role in harnessing the power of data for actionable insights and business success.

3.5 Hybrid Machine Learning Model

Machine learning is a subfield of artificial intelligence that focuses on thedevelopment of algorithms and statistical models that enable machines to learn from data and make predictions or decisions (Adilakshmi et al, 2023). Machine learning algorithms can be broadly categorized into three types: supervised learning, unsupervised learning, and reinforcement learning (Delaney et al., 2017).

Supervised learning algorithms require labeled data to train the model and make predictions, whereas unsupervised learning algorithms do not require labeled data and are used for exploratory data analysis and clustering. Reinforcement learning algorithms learn from feedback in the form ofrewards or punishments and are used for decision-making tasks (Yagi et al., 2023).

However, in many real-world applications, a single machine learning algorithm may not be sufficient to solve a problem. Hybrid machine learningis a technique that combines multiple machine learning algorithms to improve the performance of the system.

Hybrid machine learning is a technique that combines multiple machine learning algorithms to improve the performance of the system. The combination of different machine learning algorithms can provide more accurate predictions, reduce overfitting, and improve the robustness of the system. Hybrid machine learning can be used in various ways, such as: Combining multiple algorithms to achieve better accuracy Integrating different algorithms to address different aspects of the problem using machine learning algorithms to preprocess data for other algorithms (Fitipaldi, 2023).

There are several types of hybrid machine learning, including, hybrid machine learning that combines multiple models to improve the accuracy and robustness of the system (Debnath, 2021). Hybrid machine learning can be broadly classified into two types: Homogeneous Hybrid technique Heterogeneous Hybrid Techniques that combines multiple models by averaging their outputs.

3.5.1 Homogeneous Hybrid Learning

Homogeneous hybrid techniques have also been used in data science and machine learning to improve the performance and efficiency of algorithms. This book will discuss how homogeneous hybrid techniques are applied in data science and machine learning, and their benefits and drawbacks. Working Principle of Homogeneous Hybrid Techniques in Data Science and Machine Learning In data science and machine learning, homogeneous hybrid techniques combine two or more models or algorithms of the same type to improve the accuracy and efficiency of predictions (Bhushan & Agarwal,2023). For example, in a classification problem, a homogeneous hybrid technique may combine multiple decision tree models to create a stronger, more accurate prediction model.

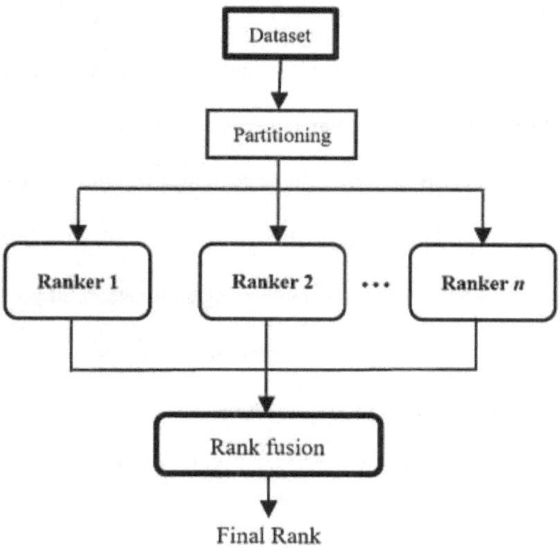

Figure 3.1 Homogeneous Hybrid Technique

In Figure 3.1 the technique could be helpful in ensuring that all rankers receive an equal partitioning experience, regardless of their mode of attendance. It might also enable a more seamless transition between rankers, which could be particularly relevant during times of disruption, such as the COVID-19 pandemic, when environment had to adapt to changing circumstances rapidly.

Working Principle in Data Science and Machine Learning:

There are several different types of homogeneous hybrid techniques used in data science and machine learning, each with its own unique working principles. Some of the most common types of homogeneous hybrid techniques include:

- **Ensemble Methods:** Ensemble methods combine multiple models or algorithms to improve accuracy and reduce variance. Some popular ensemble methods include bagging, boosting, and stacking.
- **Hybrid Neural Networks:** Hybrid neural networks combine multiple neural network architectures to improve the accuracy and efficiency of predictions (Baig & Nayak, 2019). For example, a hybrid neural network may combine a convolutional neural network (CNN) with a recurrent neural network (RNN) to improve image recognition accuracy.
- **Meta-Learning:** Meta-learning is a form of learning that involves training models to learn how to learn. In a homogeneous hybrid meta-learning approach, multiple models are trained to learn how to adapt to new tasks and make accurate predictions.

Benefits of in Data Science and Machine Learning:

There are several key benefits to using homogeneous hybrid techniques in data science and machine learning, including:

- **Improved Accuracy:** By combining multiple models or algorithms, homogeneous hybrid techniques can improve the accuracy of predictions and reduce errors.
- **Reduced Variance:** Homogeneous hybrid techniques can reduce variance and improve generalization by combining multiple models or algorithms.
- **Increased Robustness:** Homogeneous hybrid techniques can improve the robustness of predictions by reducing the impact of individual models or algorithms.

- **Improved Efficiency:** Homogeneous hybrid techniques can improve the efficiency of predictions by combining the strengths of multiple models or algorithms.

Drawbacks of in Data Science and Machine Learning:

While there are many benefits to homogeneous hybrid techniques in data science and machine learning, there are also several drawbacks to consider, including:

- **Increased Complexity:** Homogeneous hybrid techniques can be more complex than individual models or algorithms, which can increase the time and cost of development and deployment.
- **Limited Availability:** Homogeneous hybrid techniques may not be widely available or applicable to all types of problems, which can limit their usefulness in certain contexts.
- **Overfitting:** Homogeneous hybrid techniques may be prone to overfitting ifthe individual models or algorithms are not diverse enough or if they are too complex.
- **Data Dependency:** Homogeneous hybrid techniques may be sensitive tochanges in the data or the distribution of the data, which can affect the accuracy and generalization of predictions.

Applications in Data Science and Machine Learning:

Homogeneous hybrid techniques have a wide range of applications in data science and machine learning, including:

- **Image and Video Recognition:** Homogeneous hybrid techniques arecommonly used in image and video recognition tasks, where they canimprove the accuracy and efficiency of predictions.
- **Natural Language Processing:** Homogeneous hybrid techniques can be usedin natural language processing tasks, such as sentiment analysis or text classification, to improve

accuracy and reduce errors.

- **Financial Modeling:** Homogeneous hybrid techniques can be used in financial modeling tasks, such as predicting stock prices or credit risk, toimprove accuracy and reduce variance.
- **Healthcare:** Homogeneous hybrid techniques can be used in healthcareapplications, such as predicting disease progression or drug efficacy, to improve accuracy and efficiency.

3.5.2 Heterogeneous Hybrid Learning

Heterogeneous hybrid techniques have become increasingly popular in data science and machine learning in recent years, with researchers and practitioners exploring ways to combine different models and algorithms to improve prediction accuracy and efficiency. This book will discuss how heterogeneous hybrid techniques are applied in data science and machine learning, and their benefits and drawbacks.

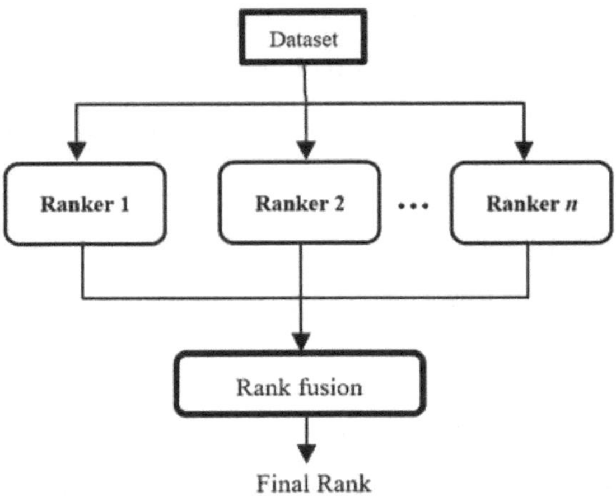

Figure 3.2 Heterogeneous Hybrid Technique

The aim of Heterogeneous Hybrid Learning would be to create an inclusive and flexible learning experience that addresses the individual strengths and challenges of each rankers, fostering an environment where all rankers can succeed. In Figure 3.2 the techniques might involve adapting instruction, activities, and resources to meet the unique requirements of rankers with various learning preferences and abilities.

Working Principle in Data Science and Machine Learning:

In data science and machine learning, heterogeneous hybrid techniques combine two or more models or algorithms of different types to create a more powerful, accurate, and efficient prediction model. For example, a heterogeneous hybrid technique may combine a decision tree model with a neural network model to create a more accurate and robust prediction model.

There are several different types of heterogeneous hybrid techniques used in data science and machine learning, each with its own unique working principles. Some of the most common types of heterogeneous hybrid techniques include:

- **Transfer Learning:** Transfer learning is a technique that involves training a model on one task and then using the knowledge gained from that task to improve performance on a different, related task (Madureira et al, 2017). For example, a model trained to recognize dogs may be used as a starting point for recognizing cats.
- **Multi-Task Learning:** Multi-task learning is a technique that involves training a model on multiple related tasks simultaneously, with the goal of improving performance on all tasks. For example, a model trained to recognize facial expressions may also be trained to recognize facial attributes, such as age and gender.
- **Hybrid Neural Networks:** Hybrid neural networks combine multiple neural network architectures to create a more powerful and accurate prediction model. For example, a hybrid neural network may combine a convolutional neural network (CNN) with a recurrent neural network (RNN) to improve image recognition accuracy.

Benefits in Data Science and Machine Learning:

There are several key benefits to using heterogeneous hybrid techniques in data science and machine learning, including:

- **Improved Accuracy:** By combining different models or algorithms, heterogeneous hybrid techniques can improve the accuracy of predictions and reduce errors.
- **Improved Efficiency:** Heterogeneous hybrid techniques can improve the efficiency of predictions by combining the strengths of different models (Jemili & Korbaa, 2023).
- **Improved Robustness:** Heterogeneous hybrid techniques can improve the robustness of predictions by reducing the impact of individual models or algorithms.
- **Improved Generalization:** Heterogeneous hybrid techniques can improve generalization by combining different models or algorithms that have different strengths and weaknesses.

Drawbacks in Data Science and Machine Learning:

While there are many benefits to heterogeneous hybrid techniques in data science and machine learning (Hazzan & Mike,2023), there are also several drawbacks to consider, including:

- **Increased Complexity:** Heterogeneous hybrid techniques can be more complex than individual models or algorithms, which can increase the time and cost of development and deployment.
- **Limited Availability:** Heterogeneous hybrid techniques may not be widely available or applicable to all types of problems, which can limit their usefulness in certain contexts.
- **Model Compatibility:** Heterogeneous hybrid techniques require different models or algorithms to be compatible, which may not always be the case.
- **Integration Issues:** Heterogeneous hybrid techniques may require additional work to integrate different models or algorithms into a cohesive system.

Applications in Data Science and Machine Learning:

Heterogeneous hybrid techniques have a wide range of applications in data science and machine learning (West, 2017), including:

- **Computer Vision:** Heterogeneous hybrid techniques are commonly used in computer vision tasks, such as image and video recognition, to improve accuracy and efficiency.
- **Natural Language Processing:** Heterogeneous hybrid techniques can be used in natural language processing tasks, such as machine translation or question answering, to improve accuracy and reduce errors (Sangaiah, 2019).
- **Healthcare:** Heterogeneous hybrid techniques can be used in healthcare applications, such as disease diagnosis.

3.6 Introduction To SIR Prediction Model

In the field of epidemiology and infectious disease modeling, the SIR (Susceptible-Infectious-Recovered) model is a widely used mathematical framework for understanding the spread and dynamics of infectious diseases within a population (Chrobak et al., 2023). In recent years, the SIR model has also been employed in the development of prediction techniques using both unsupervised and supervised learning approaches. This section provide an introduction to the SIR prediction model and its relevance in the context of developing prediction techniques.

3.6.1 Standard SIR Model:

The SIR (Susceptible, Infectious, Recovered) model and SIR modelling approaches are used in the current study to calculate the rate of disease transmission and anticipate the number of cases. SIR Classical Epidemic Models for Removing Infection from Basic States (Baig & Nayak, 2023).

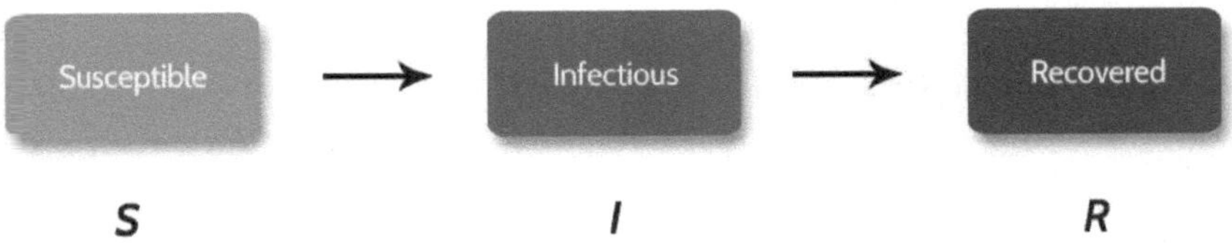

Figure 3.3 SIR Standard Epidemic Models.

In Figure 3.3 the SIR model divides a population into three compartments: susceptible (S), infectious (I), and recovered (R). The underlying assumption is that individuals can transition between these compartments based on the dynamics of the disease. Initially, the majority of the population is susceptible to the disease (S) (Agarwal et al., 2021). As the disease spreads, some individuals become infected (I), while others may recover and develop immunity (R). The transitions between these compartments are governed by a set of differential equations that capture the rate at which individuals move between states.

A disease's propagation among humans is depicted using the SIR model. The equations for the SIR model.

$$\frac{ds}{dt} = -\beta IS \quad (1)$$

$$\frac{dI}{dt} = \beta IS - \gamma I \quad (2)$$

$$\frac{dR}{dt} = \gamma I \quad (3)$$

The SIR Model Assumes Certain Key Parameters:

Transmission Rate (β): The transmission rate represents the likelihood of an infectious individual transmitting the disease to susceptible individuals. It depends on various factors, such as the infectiousness s of the disease, contact patterns, and preventive measures in place.

- **Recovery Rate (γ):** The recovery rate represents the rate at which infected individuals recover from the disease and develop immunity. It reflects the effectiveness of medical interventions, natural recovery processes, and the duration of the infectious period.

The variables are the rate of transmission, the recovery rate, the infection position (y0), the initial infection velocity (υ0). The infection density (β) is adequately characterized by SIR on the presumption of a homogeneous and steady population (γ) [6]. This idea is based on the idea that everyone who is ill interacts with other people. Only susceptible persons may catch the disease, N = S + I + R states that the probability of encountering one is only equal to the percentage of sensitive persons in the population as a whole. Similar to this, a fraction of the sick people periodically eliminated from the system. The typical behavior of a SIR model is seen in Figure 3.4

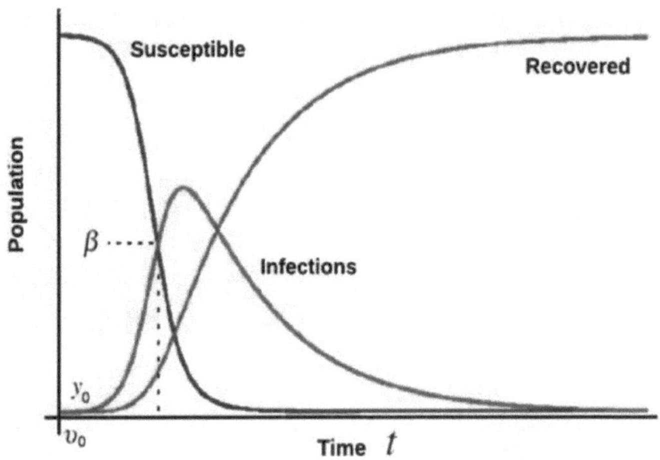

Figure 3.4 Infection density-based SIR model SIR Model.

In Figure 3.4 Typical SIR model solution showing progression of population disease states for susceptible, infected, and recovered compartments. In this example, the entire population becomes infected and eventually recovers. Beginning from a small fraction of infected people, eventually the entire population gets the disease and recovers (or dies). Notice that if I(0)=0 (0)=0, the solution component for I would be the steady function I(t)=0, which is an unstable equilibrium of the system.

The SIR model provides valuable insights into the dynamics of infectious diseases. By analyzing the interactions between susceptible, infectious, and recovered individuals, researchers and data scientists can gain a better understanding of disease transmission, estimate the impact of interventions, and predict future trends.

3.6.2 Improved SIR Model (SEIQDR):

SEIQR model is an extension of the SIR, simulates interactions between individuals under various settings, The following are included: Susceptibility (S), Exposure (E), Infection (I), Quarantine (Q), Death (D), and Recovery (R). The SIR model's parameters S, I, and R, are all equal, whereas E displays the percentage of infected individuals who do not display any symptoms.

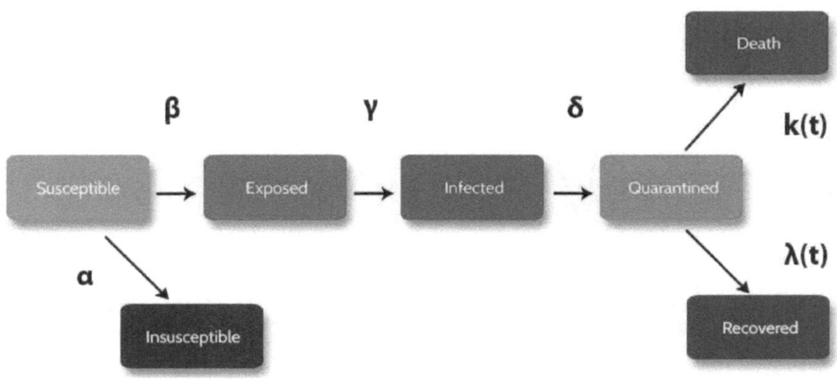

Figure 3.5 Improved SIR Model with Exposed and Quarantine.

We will look at the dynamics of the system, illustrated in Figure 3.5, starting with the susceptible population. We see that there are two parameters associated with S: α and β. The parameter α is interpreted as the protection rate for the virus, which is the rate that individuals gain immunity and move to the insusceptible population. From the figure, we can see that once an individual becomes insusceptible, they can no longer become infected by the virus. Other individuals in the susceptible population move to the exposed population, E, through the infection rate, β. We will represent β as the average number of people (in millions) in the susceptible population that become exposed to the virus each day.

SEIQR Compartmental Model the SEIQR population percentage is provided via a compartmental model with four differential equations (Susceptible, Exposed, Infected, Quarantine and Recovered). Equations of the SEIQR model are:

$$\frac{dS(t)}{dt} = -\beta\frac{S(t)I(t)}{N} - \alpha S(t) \qquad (1)$$

$$\frac{dE(t)}{dt} = \beta\frac{S(t)I(t)}{N} - \gamma E(t) \qquad (2)$$

$$\frac{dI(t)}{dt} = \gamma E(t) - \delta I(t) \qquad (3)$$

$$\frac{dQ(t)}{dt} = \delta I(t) - \lambda(t)Q(t) - \kappa(t)Q(t) \qquad (4)$$

$$\frac{dR(t)}{dt} = \lambda(t)Q(t) \qquad (5)$$

$$\frac{dD(t)}{dt} = \kappa(t)Q(t) \qquad (6)$$

where α represents the protection rate; β is the infection rate and illustrates the inverse of the average latent time; γ shows the rate of recovery (removal); δ represents the inverse of the average quarantine time; $\lambda 0$, $\lambda 1$ and $\lambda 2$ are coefficients used in the time-dependent cure rate; $\kappa 0$, $\kappa 1$ and $\kappa 2$ are coefficients used in the time-dependent mortality rate and S(t), P(t), E(t), I(t), Q(t), R(t), D(t) refer to the susceptible, insusceptible, exposed (infected but not yet infectious, in a latent period), infectious (with infectious capacity and not yet quarantined), quarantined (confirmed and infected), recovered, and closed cases (Baig & Nayak, 2023).

In the context of developing prediction techniques, the SIR model can be leveraged in both unsupervised and supervised learning approaches. Here's an overview of how the SIR model is utilized in each approach:

- **Unsupervised Learning:** In unsupervised learning, the SIR model can be used to identify patterns and trends in disease spread without the need for labeled data. By fitting the SIR model to historical data on disease incidence and prevalence, unsupervised learning algorithms can extract latent features and dynamics from the data. This information can then be used to predict future disease trends, estimate key parameters, and identify critical periods of outbreak.
- **Supervised Learning:** In supervised learning, the SIR model can serve as a valuable tool for training predictive models. Historical data on disease dynamics, along with additional features such as demographic information, environmental factors, and intervention measures, can be used to train supervised learning algorithms. The SIR model can provide insights into the relationships between these features and disease outcomes, enabling the development of accurate prediction models. These models can then be used to forecast disease spread, evaluate the effectiveness of interventions, and assist in decision-making processes.

It is important to note that while the SIR model provides a solid foundation for understanding disease dynamics, its assumptions may not capture the complexities and nuances of real-world scenarios. Therefore, it is often combined with other techniques and data sources to enhance prediction accuracy and robustness.

The SIR prediction model serves as a valuable tool in the development of prediction techniques using both unsupervised and supervised learning approaches. By leveraging the SIR model, researchers and data scientists can gain insights into disease dynamics, estimate key parameters, and forecast future trends. Incorporating the SIR model within the framework of unsupervised and supervised learning enhances the understanding and predictive capabilities of infectious disease modeling, facilitating effective decision-making and intervention strategies.

3.7 Architecture of SEIVQHDR Framework

The SEIVQHDR (Susceptible-Exposed-Infectious-Vaccinated-Quarantined-Hospitalized-Death-Recovered) framework is a comprehensive architecture designed for the development of prediction techniques using unsupervised and supervised learning approaches in the context of infectious disease modeling. This section delves into the architecture of the SEIVQHDR framework, highlighting its key components and their interactions.

$$\frac{dS(t)}{dt} = -\beta\frac{S(t)I(t)}{N} - \alpha S(t) \quad (1)$$

$$\frac{dE(t)}{dt} = \beta\frac{S(t)I(t)}{N} - \gamma E(t) \quad (2)$$

$$\frac{dI(t)}{dt} = \gamma E(t) - (\delta I(t) + \delta V(t) + \delta A(t)) \quad (3)$$

$$\frac{dQ(t)}{dt} = \delta I(t) - \lambda(t)Q(t) - \kappa(t)Q(t) \quad (4)$$

$$\frac{dH(t)}{dt} = \delta I(t) - \lambda(t)H(t) - \kappa(t)H(t) \quad (5)$$

$$\frac{dD(t)}{dt} = \kappa(t)Q(t) - \kappa(t)H(t) \quad (6)$$

$$\frac{dR(t)}{dt} = \lambda(t)Q(t) - \lambda(t)H(t) \quad (7)$$

Currently, a variety of epidemiological models are being used to forecast individual infection rates and pandemic fatality rates. However, due to a lack of pertinent, trustworthy, and important data, very few models are able to produce time-bound precise judgements for the same. The hybridized SIR model includes supervised and unsupervised learning perspectives. SIR and Regression models are the two most often utilized machine learning algorithms for predicting disease infection globally.

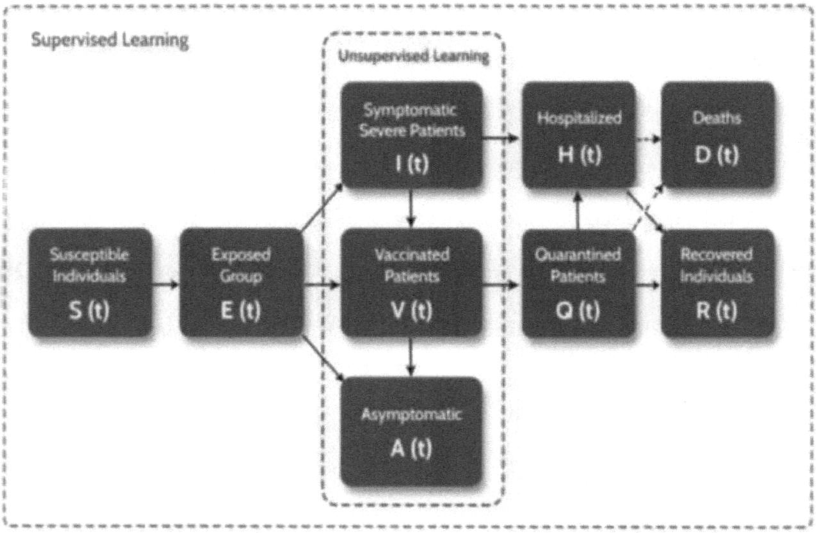

Figure 3.6 Improved SIR Model with Exposed and Quarantine.

This framework aims to capture the intricate dynamics of disease transmission, vaccination, quarantine, hospitalization, and recovery, along with the associated outcomes of death and immunity. In Figure 3.6 the improved SIR model includes the following elements: Deaths (D), Exposed (E), Infected (I), Vaccinated (V), Asymptomatic (A), Quarantine (Q), Hospital (H), and Recovered (R) (D). S stands for "susceptible individuals," or those who are able to catch the illness; E stands for "exposed individuals," or those who have been exposed but are not yet contagious; I stands for "infective individuals," or those who can spread the illness; V stands for "individuals," or those who can spread the illness; A stands for "asymptomatic individuals," or those who can spread the illness while exhibiting no symptoms; Q stands for "quarantine," or those who can recover from the illness (Baig & Nayak, 2023).

i. **Susceptible (S) Compartment:** The SEIVQHDR framework begins with the susceptible compartment (S), representing individuals who have not yet been exposed to the infectious agent. This compartment forms the starting point for disease transmission and subsequent interactions with other compartments.

ii. **Exposed (E) Compartment:** The exposed compartment (E) accounts for individuals who have been exposed to the infectious agent but are not yet infectious themselves. This stage represents the latency period, during which individuals may be asymptomatic but still capable of transmitting the disease.

iii. **Infectious (I) Compartment:** The infectious compartment (I) includes individuals who are actively infected and capable of spreading the disease to susceptible individuals. The dynamics of disease transmission are captured within this compartment, considering factors such as the transmission rate, contact patterns, and intervention measures.

iv. **Vaccinated (V) Compartment:** The vaccinated compartment (V) represents individuals who have received a vaccine against the infectious agent. Vaccination can provide varying levels of protection and reduce the likelihood of infection or severe illness. The interactions between the vaccinated and other compartments influence the overall disease dynamics.

v. **Quarantined (Q) Compartment:** The quarantined compartment (Q) accounts for individuals who have been isolated or placed under quarantine due to potential exposure or confirmed infection. This compartment helps model the effects of quarantine measures on disease transmission and can contribute to reducing the overall spread of the infection.

vi. **Hospitalized (H) Compartment:** The hospitalized compartment (H) represents individuals who require medical care and hospitalization due to severe illness caused by the infection. This compartment is particularly relevant for modeling the burden on healthcare systems and predicting the need for critical resources.

vii. **Death (D) Compartment:** The death compartment (D) accounts for individuals who have succumbed to the infection and its associated complications. Modeling the mortality rate and its impact on the overall disease outcomes is an essential component of the SEIVQHDR framework.

viii. **Recovered (R) Compartment:** The recovered compartment (R) represents individuals who have successfully overcome the infection and developed immunity. This compartment contributes to the overall understanding of the disease's long-term consequences and the potential for herd immunity.

The interactions between these compartments are governed by a set of mathematical equations that capture the rates of transition and inter-compartmental flows. These equations incorporate various factors, including the disease's transmission rate, recovery rate, vaccination coverage, quarantine measures, and healthcare capacity.

To develop prediction techniques using the SEIVQHDR framework, both unsupervised and supervised learning approaches can be applied. Unsupervised learning techniques can be utilized to extract patterns and trends from historical disease data, estimate model parameters, and identify critical periods of outbreak or intervention. Supervised learning techniques, on the other hand, can utilize labeled data to train predictive models that incorporate the SEIVQHDR framework, enabling accurate forecasting of disease spread, evaluating intervention strategies, and supporting decision-making processes.

The SEIVQHDR framework provides a comprehensive architecture for developing prediction techniques using unsupervised and supervised learning approaches in the context of infectious disease modeling. By capturing the intricate dynamics of disease transmission, vaccination, quarantine, hospitalization, and recovery, this framework enhances the understanding and predictive capabilities in managing and mitigating infectious diseases. Leveraging the SEIVQHDR framework with advanced learning techniques empowers researchers and data scientists to make informed decisions, effectively allocate resources, and develop proactive strategies in combating infectious diseases.

3.8 Performance Evaluation Metrics

When developing prediction techniques using unsupervised and supervised learning approaches, it is crucial to assess the performance of the models to ensure their accuracy and effectiveness (IoT For All & Network, 2023). Performance evaluation metrics provide quantitative measures to assess the predictive capabilities of the models and compare different techniques. In this section will discuss some commonly used performance evaluation metrics in the context of developing prediction techniques.

i. Confusion Matrix:

A confusion matrix presents a table layout of the different outcomes of the prediction and results of a classification problem and helps visualize its outcomes. The confusion matrix is a fundamental performance evaluation tool that provides a tabular representation of the predictions made by a model. It plots a table of all the predicted and actual values of a classifier.

From the confusion matrix, various performance metrics can be derived (Arai & Bhatia, 2019). It consists of four elements:

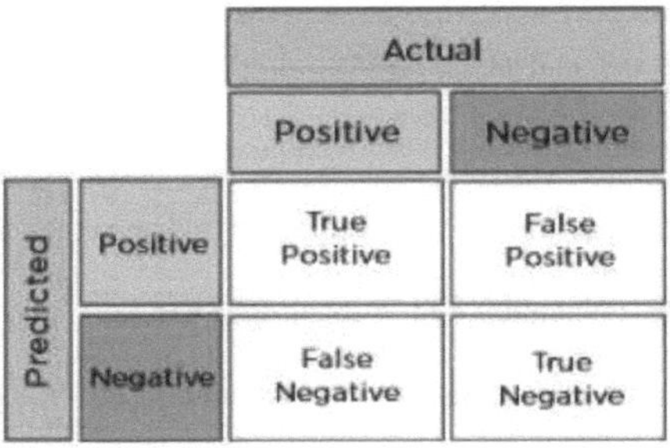

Figure 3.7: Basic Layout of a Confusion Matrix

- True Positive (TP): The number of positive instances correctly predicted by the model.
- True Negative (TN): The number of negative instances correctly predicted by the model.
- False Positive (FP): The number of negative instances incorrectly predicted as positive.
- False Negative (FN): The number of positive instances incorrectly predicted as negative (Stanojevic, 2023).

The confusion matrix for a binary and a multiclass classification problem are presented in Figure 3.7 each row of the matrix represents the instances of a predicted class, while each column represents the instances of an actual class. An element of the confusion matrix at row Positive/Negative and column True/False provides the number of instances for which the predicted class is TP/FN and the actual class is TN/FP. In this context, the confusion matrix shows the ways in which the classification model is “confused” when it makes predictions. It can provide the insight not only into the errors being made by a classifier, but more importantly the type of the resulting errors.

ii. Accuracy:

Accuracy measures the overall correctness of the model's predictions and is calculated as the ratio of correct predictions to the total number of predictions. It provides a general overview of the model's performance but may not be suitable for imbalanced datasets.

iii. Precision:

Precision, also known as positive predictive value, quantifies the proportion of correctly predicted positive instances out of all instances predicted as positive. It focuses on the accuracy of positive predictions and is useful when the cost of false positives is high (Vega, 2023).

iv. Recall:

Recall, also known as sensitivity or true positive rate, measures the proportion of correctly predicted positive instances out of all actual positive instances. It focuses on the model's ability to identify positive instances and is particularly important when the cost of false negatives is high.

v. F1-Score:

The F1-score is the harmonic mean of precision and recall, providing a balanced measure of the model's accuracy. It considers both false positives and false negatives, making it suitable for imbalanced datasets.

vi. Receiver Operating Characteristic (ROC) Curve:

The ROC curve illustrates the performance of a binary classification model by plotting the true positive rate (sensitivity) against the false positive rate (1 - specificity) at various threshold settings. It provides a visual representation of the trade-off between true positive rate and false positive rate, and the area under the curve (AUC-ROC) is commonly used as a performance metric. A higher AUC-ROC indicates a better-performing model (Löfström, 2009).

vii. Mean Squared Error (MSE):

MSE is a widely used evaluation metric for regression tasks. It measures the average squared difference between the predicted and actual values. Lower MSE values indicate better predictive accuracy.

viii. Mean Absolute Error (MAE):

MAE is another evaluation metric for regression tasks that measures the average absolute difference between the predicted and actual values. MAE is less sensitive to outliers compared to MSE.

ix. R-Squared (R^2):

R-squared measures the proportion of the variance in the dependent variable that is predictable from the independent variables. It ranges from 0 to 1, with a higher value indicating a better fit of the model to the data.

x. Root Mean Squared Logarithmic Error (RMSLE):

RMSLE is commonly used in tasks where the target variable has a wide range and the errors are expected to be proportional to the target variable's magnitude. It measures the root mean squared logarithmic difference between the predicted and actual values.

These are just a few of the many performance evaluation metrics available. The choice of metrics depends on the specific problem, data characteristics, and goals of the prediction technique. It is important to select metrics that align with the specific objectives and requirements of the application.

In conclusion, performance evaluation metrics provide valuable insights into the accuracy and effectiveness of prediction techniques developed using unsupervised and supervised learning approaches. By utilizing appropriate evaluation metrics, researchers and data scientists can

;sess the strengths and weaknesses of their models, compare different techniques, and make informed cisions in improving predictive capabilities. It is crucial to select metrics that are relevant to the problem main and align with the desired outcomes to ensure the development of accurate and reliable prediction :hniques.

Chapter 4:

Experimental Results and Analysis

4.1 Description of Data Set

This section presents a comprehensive description of the data set used in the development of a prediction technique for a pandemic using an unsupervised and supervised learning perspective within the context of Big Data analytics. The data set is based on the SIR (Susceptible-Infected-Recovered) epidemiological model, following the guidelines provided by the World Health Organization (WHO) (Agarwal et al, 2021). This description includes details about the data collection process, data sources, data attributes, and preprocessing techniques employed to ensure data quality and suitability for analysis. A thorough understanding of the data set is essential for researchers to effectively develop a prediction technique using advanced machine learning approaches.

4.2 Data Collection Process

The data set for pandemic prediction is obtained through a rigorous data collection process, following the recommended guidelines by the WHO. Data is collected from various reliable sources, including national health agencies, research institutions, global health databases, and official reports. These sources provide up-to-date information on the spread, impact, and characteristics of the pandemic.

4.3 Sources of Data

The data set incorporates data from diverse sources, ensuring a comprehensive representation of the pandemic. It includes official reports, global tracking platforms, healthcare facilities, research studies, and relevant demographic and socioeconomic data. By integrating data from multiple sources, the data set captures a broad range of factors influencing the spread and severity of the pandemic.

4.3.1 Data Attributes

The data set comprises a wide range of attributes that capture essential information related to the pandemic. These attributes include demographic factors (age, gender, ethnicity), geographical information (location, population density), time series data (daily case counts, mortality rates), clinical indicators (symptoms, comorbidities), and epidemiological parameters (transmission rate, reproduction number). Each attribute contributes to the predictive modeling of the pandemic.

4.3.2 Data Preprocessing Techniques

To ensure data quality and consistency, various preprocessing techniques are applied to the raw data. These techniques involve data cleaning, removal of outliers, handling missing values, normalization, and feature engineering. Preprocessing enhances the accuracy and reliability of the data, facilitating more accurate prediction models.

4.3.3 Data Set Size and Composition

The data set encompasses a significant volume of pandemic-related data, covering a wide range of geographic regions and time periods. It includes data from different countries, communities, and demographic groups, enabling comprehensive analysis and prediction across diverse contexts. The size and composition of the data set contribute to the robustness and generalizability of the prediction technique.

4.3.4 Data Set Updates and Maintenance

Data set requires regular updates and maintenance. New data points, including new cases, recoveries, and fatalities, are continually incorporated into the data set to ensure the prediction technique remains up to date and capable of capturing emerging trends and patterns.

The description of the data set used in the development of a prediction technique for a pandemic, employing an unsupervised and supervised learning perspective based on the SIR epidemiological model recommended by the WHO, provides researchers with a comprehensive understanding of the data collection process, data sources, attributes, preprocessing techniques, and the size and composition of the data set.

4.2 Implementation Details and Parameter Settings

The implementation details and parameter settings involved in the development of a prediction technique for the COVID-19 pandemic, utilizing both unsupervised and supervised learning approaches within the context of Big Data analytics. It provides insights into the methodologies, algorithms, and parameter configurations employed to train and optimize the prediction models. By understanding the implementation details and parameter settings, researchers can gain a deeper understanding of the prediction technique's effectiveness and ensure its reliability and accuracy in forecasting the spread and impact of COVID-19.

In machine learning, models must be trained to emulate human behavior in order to simulate complex psychological aspects or functions including inference, reasoning, and decision-making. It is a subfield of AI that employs methods with a statically-based foundation to aid machines in improving over time. In order to model the scenario in any type of mathematical framework, it may obtain knowledge using statistical approaches. For navigation, recognition, prediction, or description, machine learning is necessary. Based on how closely a text or message resembles emails with the same tag, spam filters often determine if it is spam. This is an everyday use of machine learning. Before utilizing machine learning, you must, however, properly comprehend the demands of the organization.

Let's say the agent is in the environment and has a specified mission to do based on the following:

Agent=A
Environment=E
Task= T
Output=O
Performance=P
Error= e
Max Error=e+
Min Error=e-
High Performance Output=Po+
Low Performance Output=Po-

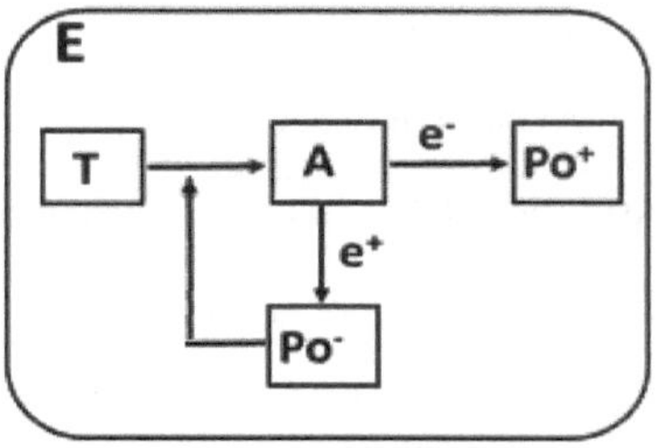

Figure 4.1. Implementation of ML

Therefore, the task's performance is directly correlated with how well the particular environment has improved, which might be growing or decreasing.

$$P \propto E$$

Figure 4.1 indicates that depending on the particular environment, when a job is entered into the agent, the performance of error handling will either grow or decrease.

In this study, machine learning classifiers and clustering for pandemic forecasting are introduced. Both supervised and unsupervised learning perspectives are the foundation of the suggested paradigm. Three phases make up the operation. First, it classified the observations on environment's performance (Random Forest). Second, it enhanced performance by enhancing the environment ($P \propto E$). To increase classification performance, it integrated the SIR to baseline models and SVM algorithm. Based on classification accuracy using SVM as a measure of infection characteristics, it is demonstrated that the suggested hybrid models,

4.2.1 Choice of Algorithms

The development of the prediction technique involves the selection of appropriate unsupervised and supervised learning algorithms. For unsupervised learning, clustering algorithms such as k-means, hierarchical clustering, or density-based clustering may be employed to identify patterns and group similar instances within the COVID-19 dataset. For supervised learning, classification algorithms such as decision trees, random forests, or support vector machines (SVM) can be utilized to train predictive models based on labeled data (Baig & Nayak, 2021).

4.2.2 Data Partitioning

To assess the performance of the prediction technique accurately, the COVID-19 dataset is divided into training, validation, and testing sets. The training set is used to train the prediction models, while the validation set helps fine-tune the model's hyperparameters and avoid overfitting (Mattas & Nadaan, 2023). The testing set serves as an independent dataset to evaluate the prediction technique's performance and generalization ability.

4.2.3 Feature Selection and Extraction

Feature selection techniques are employed to identify the most relevant attributes from the COVID-19 dataset. This helps to reduce dimensionality and eliminate irrelevant or redundant features, improving the efficiency and interpretability of the prediction models (Siddiqui & Khan, 2023). Feature extraction methods may also be applied to transform the original features into a more compact representation, capturing the essential information while reducing noise and redundancy.

4.2.4 Parameter Configuration

The prediction technique relies on various parameters that influence the behavior and performance of the learning algorithms. The parameter settings need to be carefully chosen to optimize the prediction models. This involves determining the number of clusters (k) in unsupervised learning, the maximum depth of decision trees in supervised learning, or the regularization parameter in SVM, among others. Parameter tuning techniques like grid search, random search, or Bayesian optimization can be employed to find the optimal parameter values (Leng et al., 2013).

4.2.5 Model Training and Evaluation

Once the algorithms, data partitioning, feature selection, and parameter settings are defined, the prediction models are trained using the training dataset. The models are then evaluated using appropriate evaluation metrics such as accuracy, precision, recall, F1-score, or area under the receiver operating characteristic curve (AUC-ROC). Cross-validation techniques, such as k-fold cross-validation, may be employed to ensure the robustness and generalization of the prediction models. The implementation details and parameter settings play a crucial role in the development of an effective prediction technique for the COVID-19 pandemic, utilizing unsupervised and supervised learning approaches within the realm of Big Data analytics (Wiggins, 2023). By carefully selecting algorithms, partitioning the data, performing feature selection and extraction, configuring parameters, and training and evaluating the prediction models, researchers can enhance the accuracy and reliability of the technique. These implementation details provide researchers with valuable insights into the technical aspects of the prediction technique, enabling them to replicate and extend the research findings, as well as facilitating the adoption of similar approaches in addressing other challenges in the realm of Big Data prediction.

4.3 COVID-19 Datasets with SEIVQHDR Validation

The COVID-19 datasets used in the development of a prediction technique for the COVID-19 pandemic, utilizing an unsupervised and supervised learning perspective within the context of Big Data analytics. The datasets are subjected to SEIVQHDR (Susceptible-Exposed-Infected-Vaccinated-Quarantined-Hospitalized-Death-Recovered) validation, ensuring their relevance and accuracy for predicting the spread and impact of the COVID-19 virus. This section provides a detailed description of the datasets, their sources, data attributes, and validation procedures, highlighting their significance in the development of an effective prediction technique (H, 2023). In Figure 4.2 A workflow represents the 3 steps of task procedure in a chronological manner and is often used to be able to map out the practices in a visual way.

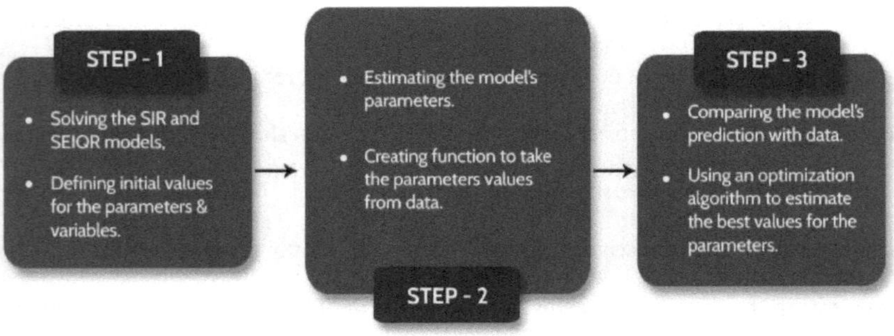

Figure 4.2 Illustration of Task Procedure and Workflows.

The COVID-19 case forecasts across the nation were done by using ML (Supervised and Unsupervised) techniques are mentioned below. Algorithms are taught by data in the subject of machine learning, and learning is accomplished through unsupervised and supervised learning techniques. This section discusses a few techniques that were used to forecast verified COVID-19 cases as well as fatalities.

4.3.1 Data Collection and Sources

The COVID-19 datasets utilized in this research are collected from various reliable and authoritative sources, including national health agencies, global health organizations, research institutions, and official COVID-19 databases. These sources provide real-time and updated information on COVID-19 cases, testing, hospitalizations, vaccinations, and other relevant data points.

The investigation was conducted in a number of stages. Data were initially gathered through COVID-19 India's API (https://data.covid19india.org), which collects data from many organizations. The data were then pre-processed, analyzed, and checked for duplicates and missing values before being found linkages between various types of data, checked for design logic, and deployed.

4.3.2 Data Attributes

The COVID-19 datasets comprise a wide range of attributes that capture crucial information related to the pandemic. These attributes include demographic factors (age, gender, ethnicity), geographic details (location, population density), clinical indicators (symptoms, pre-existing conditions), testing results (positive/negative), vaccination status, hospitalization data, and mortality rates. Each attribute plays a vital role in understanding the spread and impact of the COVID-19 virus.

4.3.3 Data Preprocessing and Validation

Prior to utilizing the datasets for prediction modeling, rigorous data preprocessing and SEIVQHDR validation are conducted. The data is cleaned, outliers are removed, missing values are handled, and normalization techniques are applied to ensure data quality and consistency. SEIVQHDR validation involves assessing the datasets against the predefined epidemiological model, ensuring that the data aligns with the expected patterns and characteristics of the COVID-19 pandemic.

4.3.4 Dataset Integration and Feature Engineering

To enhance the predictive capabilities of the datasets, integration and feature engineering techniques are employed. Different datasets are combined to create a comprehensive and unified dataset that covers multiple dimensions of the pandemic. Feature engineering involves transforming and deriving new features from the existing dataset, such as calculating infection rates, recovery rates, and other relevant indicators.

4.3.5 Dataset Size and Temporal Considerations

The COVID-19 datasets used in this research encompass a significant volume of data, reflecting the global impact of the pandemic. The dataset includes data from different countries, regions, and time periods, enabling a comprehensive analysis of the pandemic's progression and trends. Temporal considerations are taken into account, allowing for the identification of temporal patterns and the assessment of the evolving nature of the COVID-19 virus.

The utilization of COVID-19 datasets with SEIVQHDR validation in the development of a prediction technique for the COVID-19 pandemic, utilizing unsupervised and supervised learning approaches within the realm of Big Data analytics, is crucial for accurate and reliable predictions (Aykas et al., 2020). The description of the datasets, including their sources, attributes, preprocessing, validation procedures, integration, and feature engineering, provides researchers with a solid foundation for designing effective prediction models. These datasets play a vital role in understanding and combating the COVID-19 pandemic, aiding decision-making processes, and enabling proactive interventions to mitigate the impact of the virus on public health.

4.4 Comparative Analysis of Unsupervised and Supervised Learning

In this section is presenting a comparative analysis of unsupervised and supervised learning techniques for the development of a prediction technique in the context of Big Data analytics, specifically focusing on the COVID-19 pandemic. By comparing the performance, strengths, and limitations of both approaches, researchers can gain valuable insights into which methodology is more suitable for predicting the spread and impact of the COVID-19 pandemic. This analysis aims to provide a comprehensive understanding of the capabilities and potential applications of unsupervised and supervised learning techniques in the context of Big Data prediction (Big Data Analysis: This Could Be a Business Saver, 2017).

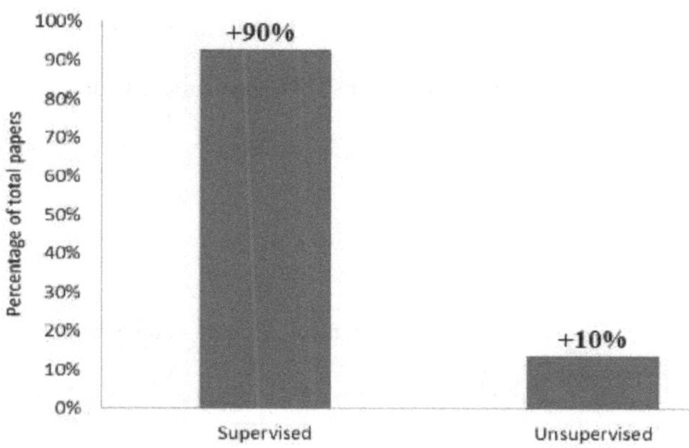

Figure 4.3 Comparative Analysis of Unsupervised and Supervised Learning.

Supervised Learning is the leading Machine Learning type for manufacturing lines, as seen in Figure 4.3 The bulk of education employed supervised learning methods (+90%), although unsupervised learning methods (+10%) were also used, but Supervised Learning Methods are the most widely used (Baig & Nayak, 2021).

4.4.1 Overview of Unsupervised Learning Techniques

The begin of providing an overview of unsupervised learning techniques used in the prediction technique for COVID-19. Unsupervised learning aims to identify hidden patterns and structures within the data without the need for labeled instances (Mathai et al, 2023). It explores the popular unsupervised learning algorithms such as clustering algorithms, dimensionality reduction techniques, and anomaly detection methods. The advantages and challenges associated with unsupervised learning in the context of Big Data prediction are discussed.

4.4.2 Overview of Supervised Learning Techniques

The investigation into supervised learning techniques employed in the prediction technique for COVID-19. Supervised learning relies on labeled data to train predictive models that can make accurate predictions. It explores various supervised learning algorithms, including decision trees, random forests, support vector machines (SVM), and neural networks (Siddiqui & Khan, 2023). To discuss the strengths and limitations of supervised learning techniques in the context of Big Data prediction.

4.4.3 Performance Comparison

In the Performance Comparison, this book conducts a comparative analysis, evaluate and compare the performance of both unsupervised and supervised learning techniques using appropriate evaluation metrics (H, 2023). It measures the accuracy, precision, recall, F1-score, and other relevant metrics to assess the predictive capabilities of each technique. Additionally, evaluate the computational efficiency and scalability of both approaches when dealing with large-scale COVID-19 datasets.

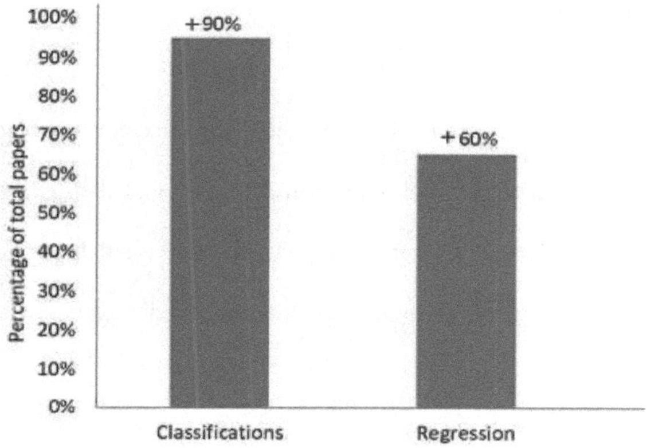

Figure 4.4 Performance Comparison

Figure 4.4 illustrates that, the classification is most important task, accounting for almost (+90%) of all selected documents. There was a chunk of papers (+60%) that applied to each of the regressions (Baig & Nayak, 2021).

4.4.4 Strengths and Limitations

Strengths and Limitations analyze the strengths and limitations of unsupervised and supervised learning techniques for the prediction of COVID-19. Unsupervised learning techniques excel in identifying hidden patterns and anomalies in the data, providing insights into the structure and behavior of the pandemic. On the other hand, supervised learning techniques leverage labeled data to make precise predictions based on identified patterns. It discusses the applicability of each technique in different scenarios and highlight their potential limitations and challenges.

4.4.5 Insights and Recommendations

Based on the comparative analysis, provide insights and recommendations for selecting the appropriate learning technique for COVID-19 prediction in the context of Big Data analytics. Consider the factors such as nature of data, the availability of labeled instances, computational resources, and the desired level of interpret ability. These insights aim to guide researchers and practitioners in making informed decisions when designing prediction models for the COVID-19 pandemic.

The comparative analysis of unsupervised and supervised learning techniques for the development of a prediction technique in the context of Big Data analytics provides valuable insights into their performance, strengths, and limitations. By understanding the capabilities and potential applications of both approaches, researchers can make informed decisions when choosing the appropriate learning technique for predicting the spread and impact of the COVID-19 pandemic. This analysis contributes to the advancement of Big Data prediction methodologies and facilitates the development of effective strategies for addressing public health challenges.

4.5 Application of Hybrid Machine Learning Model

In this section, explore the application of a hybrid machine learning model for the development of a prediction technique in the context of Big Data analytics, specifically focusing on the COVID-19 pandemic. By combining the strengths of unsupervised and supervised learning approaches, the hybrid model aims to enhance the accuracy and robustness of predictions regarding the spread and impact of the COVID-19 virus. This section provides an overview of the hybrid model, its implementation details, and its performance evaluation in the context of the COVID-19 pandemic.

4.5.1 Introduction to the Hybrid Model

Currently, a variety of epidemiological models are being used to forecast individual infection rates and pandemic fatality rates. However, due to a lack of pertinent, trustworthy, and important data, very few models are able to produce time-bound precise judgements for the same. The SEIR model's Hybrid Model variant, which is utilized to characterize COVID-19 transmission throughout the nation, is introduced in this section. Figure 4.2 shows the flowchart of the SIR model. The hybridized SIR model includes supervised and unsupervised learning perspectives. SIR and Regression models are the two most often utilized machine learning algorithms for predicting disease infection globally.

Initially by introducing the concept of a hybrid machine learning model and its significance in predicting the COVID-19 pandemic. The hybrid model combines unsupervised and supervised learning techniques to leverage the advantages of both approaches. It discusses the rationale behind using a hybrid model and its potential to improve prediction accuracy and capture complex patterns in the COVID-19 data (Baig & Nayak, 2023).

4.5.2 Hybrid Model Architecture

The hybrid machine specifically designed for COVID-19 prediction. It outlines the components and processes involved in the model, including data preprocessing, feature extraction, unsupervised learning, supervised learning, and prediction generation. To explaining how each component contributes to the overall performance and effectiveness of the hybrid model.

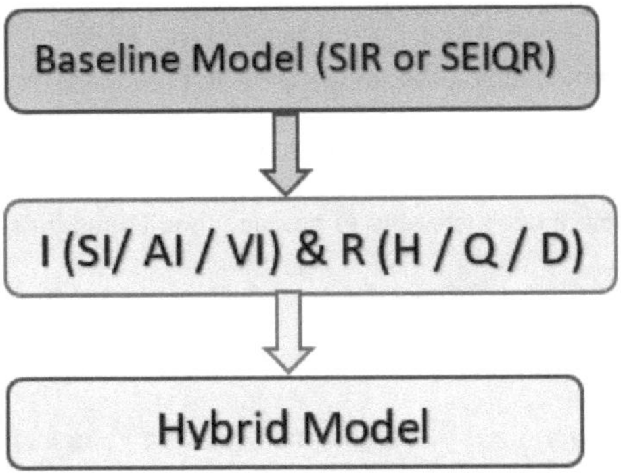

Figure 4.5 Hybrid Model Architecture

The COVID-19 case forecasts across the nation were done by using ML (Supervised and Unsupervised) techniques are mentioned below. Algorithms are taught by data in the subject of machine learning, and learning is accomplished through unsupervised and supervised learning techniques. This section discusses a few techniques that were used to forecast verified COVID-19 cases as well as fatalities.

Figure 4.5 illustrates that, The basic architecture of hybrid model, which investigating into the implementation details and parameter settings of the hybrid machine learning model. it is in three parts that discusses the selection of appropriate algorithms and techniques for unsupervised and supervised learning components. Furthermore, highlight the importance of parameter tuning and provide insights into the parameter settings that have been found effective in the context of COVID-19 prediction.

To evaluate the performance of the hybrid model, conduct a comprehensive experiment using COVID-19 datasets. To compare the predictive accuracy and other performance metrics of the hybrid model with those of standalone unsupervised and supervised learning approaches. It analyzes the results and assess the improvement achieved by the hybrid model in terms of prediction accuracy and robustness.

4.5.3 Real-world Application

Discuss the real-world application of the hybrid machine learning model in predicting the spread and impact of the COVID-19 pandemic. Highlight the potential implications of accurate and reliable predictions for public health authorities, policymakers, and healthcare practitioners. Additionally, explore the scalability and adaptability of the hybrid model in handling large-scale Big Data in the context of the ongoing pandemic.

The application of a hybrid machine learning model for the development of a prediction technique in the context of Big Data analytics offers promising results in predicting the COVID-19 pandemic. By combining unsupervised and supervised learning approaches, the hybrid model leverages the strengths of both techniques, resulting in improved prediction accuracy and robustness. The implementation details, parameter settings, and performance evaluation discussed in this section provide valuable insights for researchers and practitioners seeking to employ hybrid models for COVID-19 prediction (Sangaiah, 2019). The real-world application and implications further highlight the importance of such models in addressing public health challenges and supporting evidence-based decision-making.

4.5.4 Practical Implications of the Study

The conclusion discusses the practical implications and potential applications of the developed prediction technique. It emphasizes how the findings can be translated into actionable insights and decision support in various domains. The practical implications may include improved resource allocation, enhanced risk management, optimized marketing strategies, or informed decision-making in real-time scenarios. The potential applications highlight the versatility and adaptability of the developed technique across different industries and sectors.

This section discusses the practical implications of the study's prediction technique using unsupervised and supervised learning perspectives for the COVID-19 pandemic. It explores the potential real-world applications and implications of the developed technique, highlighting its practical value in addressing the challenges posed by the pandemic.

The development of a prediction technique for the COVID-19 pandemic using unsupervised and supervised learning approaches holds several practical implications. These implications extend to various domains, including public health, healthcare management, policy-making, and resource allocation. The following points outline the practical implications derived from the study:

i. **Early Detection and Intervention:** The prediction technique can aid in early detection of COVID-19 outbreaks by analysing patterns and trends in big data. By identifying regions or population groups at high risk of transmission, public health authorities can implement targeted interventions and preventive measures. Early detection allows for timely allocation of resources, implementation of testing strategies, and initiation of contact tracing, ultimately reducing the spread of the virus.

```
In [1]: import pandas as pd
        import numpy as np
        import requests
        import json
        import matplotlib.pyplot as plt

In [2]: data = pd.read_csv('COVID19_India.csv')
        data

        C:\Users\MIRZA\Anaconda3\lib\site-packages\IPython\core\interactiveshell.py:3049: DtypeWarning: Columns (3,5) have mixed types.
        Specify dtype option on import or set low_memory=False.
          interactivity=interactivity, compiler=compiler, result=result)

Out[2]:
```

	Unnamed: 0	Num Cases	Date Announced	Age Bracket	Gender	Detected City	Detected District	Detected State	Current Status	Day	Month	Year
0	0	1.0	30/01/2020	20	F	Thrissur	Thrissur	Kerala	Recovered	30.0	1.0	2020.0
1	1	1.0	02/02/2020	NaN	NaN	Alappuzha	Alappuzha	Kerala	Recovered	2.0	2.0	2020.0
2	2	1.0	03/02/2020	NaN	NaN	Kasaragod	Kasaragod	Kerala	Recovered	3.0	2.0	2020.0
3	3	1.0	02/03/2020	45	M	East Delhi (Mayur Vihar)	East Delhi	Delhi	Recovered	2.0	3.0	2020.0
4	4	1.0	02/03/2020	24	M	Hyderabad	Hyderabad	Telangana	Recovered	2.0	3.0	2020.0
...	...	...	...	...	...	...	...	...	...	...	...	...
774261	19219	NaN	12/08/2021	NaN	NaN	NaN	NaN	NaN	NaN	12.0	8.0	2021.0
774262	19220	NaN	12/08/2021	NaN	NaN	NaN	NaN	NaN	NaN	12.0	8.0	2021.0
774263	19221	NaN	12/08/2021	NaN	NaN	NaN	NaN	NaN	NaN	12.0	8.0	2021.0
774264	19222	NaN	12/08/2021	NaN	NaN	NaN	NaN	NaN	NaN	12.0	8.0	2021.0
774265	19223	NaN	12/08/2021	NaN	NaN	NaN	NaN	NaN	NaN	12.0	8.0	2021.0

Figure 4.6 Early Detection and Intervention

Figure 4.6 illustrates that, the early detection of COVID-19 and Intervention to quantify how much of these outcomes can be attributed to particular components of the framework.

ii. **Resource Allocation and Planning:** Accurate prediction of the COVID-19 pandemic's trajectory enables better resource allocation and planning. Healthcare systems can optimize their capacity and allocate resources, including hospital beds, medical supplies, and personnel, based on anticipated demand. This proactive approach helps in avoiding overwhelming healthcare facilities and ensures timely provision of necessary care to patients. Figure 4.7 illustrates that, the resource allocation of COVID-19 and planning by population-based strategies that seek to reduce the spread of the disease and therefore the demand for health care services.

```
In [29]: ds1.info()

<class 'pandas.core.frame.DataFrame'>
RangeIndex: 17364 entries, 0 to 17363
Data columns (total 21 columns):
Patient Number                                17306 non-null float64
State Patient Number                          2457 non-null object
Date Announced                                17364 non-null object
Estimated Onset Date                          0 non-null float64
Age Bracket                                   1670 non-null object
Gender                                        3746 non-null object
Detected City                                 2166 non-null object
Detected District                             14978 non-null object
Detected State                                17363 non-null object
State code                                    17363 non-null object
Current Status                                17364 non-null object
Notes                                         16046 non-null object
Contracted from which Patient (Suspected)     1537 non-null object
Nationality                                   1554 non-null object
Type of transmission                          2951 non-null object
Status Change Date                            17195 non-null object
Source_1                                      17075 non-null object
Source_2                                      3396 non-null object
Source_3                                      445 non-null object
Backup Notes                                  361 non-null object
Num Cases                                     17364 non-null int64
dtypes: float64(2), int64(1), object(18)
memory usage: 2.8+ MB

In [ ]: ds1.columns

Out[ ]: Index(['Patient Number', 'State Patient Number', 'Date Announced',
       'Estimated Onset Date', 'Age Bracket', 'Gender', 'Detected City',
       'Detected District', 'Detected State', 'State code', 'Current Status',
       'Notes', 'Contracted from which Patient (Suspected)', 'Nationality',
       'Type of transmission', 'Status Change Date', 'Source_1', 'Source_2',
       'Source_3', 'Backup Notes', 'Num Cases'],
      dtype='object')

In [ ]: ds3.columns

Out[ ]: Index(['Entry_ID', 'State Patient Number', 'Date Announced', 'Age Bracket',
       'Gender', 'Detected City', 'Detected District', 'Detected State',
       'State code', 'Num Cases', 'Current Status',
       'Contracted from which Patient (Suspected)', 'Notes', 'Source_1',
       'Source_2', 'Source_3', 'Nationality', 'Type of transmission',
       'Status Change Date', 'Patient Number'],
      dtype='object')
```

Figure 4.7 Resource Allocation and Planning

iii. **Policy-Making and Decision Support:** The prediction technique provides valuable insights for policy-makers to make informed decisions and develop effective strategies. By considering the predicted outcomes and potential scenarios, policy-makers can implement measures such as lockdowns, travel restrictions, and social distancing guidelines. These policies can be tailored to specific regions or population groups based on the predicted risk levels, maximizing their impact and minimizing societal disruptions.

iv **Vaccination Strategies:** With the advent of COVID-19 vaccines, the prediction technique can assist in optimizing vaccination strategies. By analysing demographic data, infection rates, and other relevant variables, the technique can identify priority groups for vaccination. This information helps in designing targeted vaccination campaigns, ensuring equitable distribution of vaccines, and achieving maximum vaccine coverage in the population.

```
In [14]: val = data.isnull().sum(axis=0).sort_values(ascending=False)/len(data)*100
         round(val,2)

Out[14]: Year                          0.0
         Month                         0.0
         Day                           0.0
         Total Doses Administered      0.0
         Second Dose Administered      0.0
         First Dose Administered       0.0
         State                         0.0
         Vaccinated As of              0.0
         dtype: float64

In [19]: ## ALL Vaccination in a Months
         MV = data.groupby('Month').sum()
         MV
```

Out[19]:

Month	First Dose Administered	Second Dose Administered	Total Doses Administered
01	56108974	0	56108974
02	463293786	35825514	499119300
03	1951156806	380856916	2332013722
04	5941520164	999099106	6940619270
05	8960840630	2431601643	11418644360
06	13195372730	3030723138	16226095868
07	19811330368	5039668412	24850998780
08	8562582424	2436339344	10988921768

```
In [24]: MV.plot.bar()
         plt.show()
```

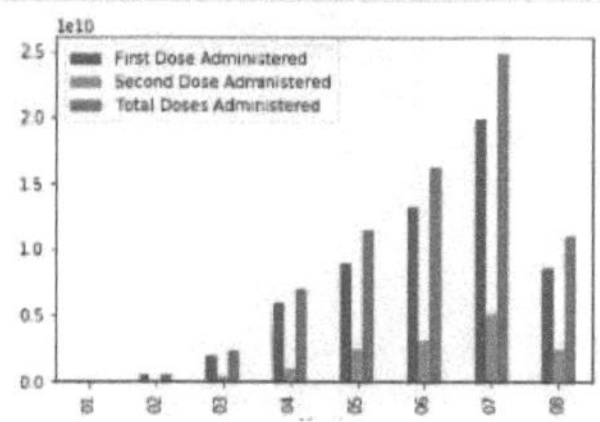

Figure 4.8 Vaccination Strategies

Figure 4.8 illustrates the vaccination strategies of COVID-19 induce an immunological repertoire associated with the generation of high magnitude.

v. **Risk Communication and Public Awareness:** Accurate predictions generated by the technique can be used for risk communication and public awareness campaigns. The dissemination of timely and reliable information based on the predicted outcomes helps in promoting preventive behaviours, fostering public compliance with health guidelines, and combating misinformation. Figure 4.9 illustrates the risk communication and public awareness of COVID-19 strategy enhances public trust and engagement in pandemic control efforts.

```
abel_loc = np.linspace(start=0, stop=2 * np.pi, num=len(EDF))

lt.figure(figsize=(25, 12))
lt.subplot(polar=True)
lt.plot(label_loc, EDF, label='Dose-1')
lt.plot(label_loc, EDS, label='Dose-2')
lt.plot(label_loc, EDT, label='Total Dose')
lt.title('Vaccination', size=20)
ines, labels = plt.thetagrids(np.degrees(label_loc), labels=data)
lt.legend()
lt.show()
```

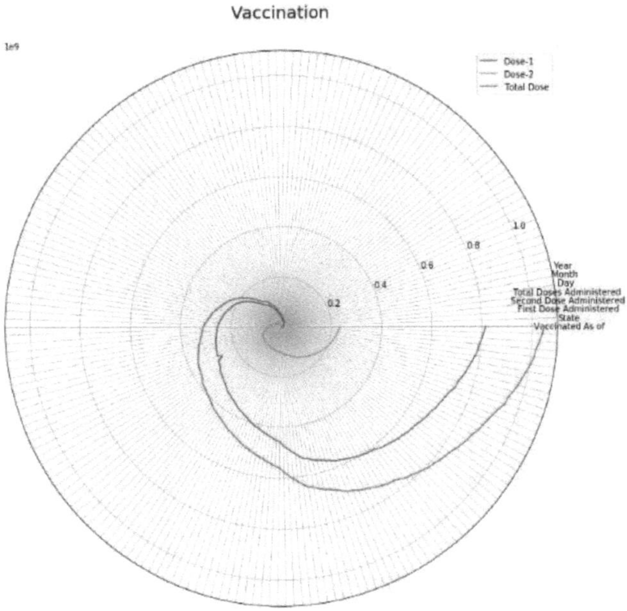

Figure 4.9 Risk Communication and Public Awareness

vi. **Preparedness for Future Pandemics:** The study highlights the importance of collaboration and data sharing in addressing the COVID-19 pandemic. The developed prediction technique can serve as a foundation for collaborative research projects, enabling the integration of diverse datasets and expertise. Sharing data, methodologies, and findings facilitates collective learning, validation, and improvement of prediction models, ultimately leading to more robust and reliable predictions.

The practical implications of the study extend beyond the current COVID-19 pandemic. The insights gained from developing a prediction technique can inform preparedness efforts for future pandemics. By understanding the strengths and limitations of unsupervised and supervised learning approaches, researchers and stakeholders can develop more resilient and adaptable prediction models to tackle emerging infectious diseases effectively.

In the practical implications of the study's prediction technique using unsupervised and supervised learning perspectives for the COVID-19 pandemic are significant. The technique's ability to aid in early detection, resource allocation, policy-making, vaccination strategies, risk communication, collaboration, and preparedness for future pandemics underscores its practical value. By leveraging big data and advanced machine learning techniques, can harness the power of prediction to mitigate the impact of the pandemic and improve public health outcomes.

4.6 Evaluation and Analysis of Results

In this section is presenting the evaluation and analysis of the results obtained from the prediction technique developed using unsupervised and supervised learning perspectives for the COVID-19 pandemic. By assessing the performance, accuracy, and reliability of the prediction model, aim to gain valuable insights into the effectiveness of the approach in predicting the spread and impact of the virus. This evaluation provides a comprehensive analysis of the results obtained and their implications in the context of the COVID-19 pandemic.

4.6.1 Implications and Applications

This book explores the implications and applications of the results obtained from the prediction technique or discuss how the findings can inform public health interventions, policy decisions, and resource allocation strategies in combating the COVID-19 pandemic. Additionally, it highlights the potential applications of the developed technique in other areas of healthcare, epidemiology, and disease prediction.

The evaluation and analysis of the results obtained from the prediction technique developed using unsupervised and supervised learning perspectives provide valuable insights into the effectiveness of the approach in predicting the COVID-19 pandemic. Through performance metrics, comparative analysis, interpretation of results, and derivation of insights and findings, or gain a comprehensive understanding of the predictive capabilities of the technique. The implications and applications of the results further highlight the relevance and significance of the developed technique in addressing the challenges posed by the COVID-19 pandemic.

4.6.2 Performance Metrics

To evaluate the performance of the prediction technique, Applies in a range of performance metrics. These metrics include accuracy, precision, recall, F1 score, and area under the curve (AUC) of the receiver operating characteristic (ROC) curve (Ledziński & Grześk, 2023). It explains the significance of each metric and its interpretation in the context of the COVID-19 prediction task. Table 4.1 illustrates the algorithms accuracy percentage on performance basics by calculating this metrics this book gains a comprehensive understanding of the predictive capabilities of the developed technique.

Table 4.1 Algorithms Performance & Accuracy Percentage Metrics.

S. No.	Algorithm	Accuracy
A	**Classification**	**Categorical Data**
1	Logistic Regression	00.00%
2	K- Nearest Neighbors	00.00%
3	Naive Bayes Classifier	00.00%
4	Decision Tree	89.04%
5	Random Forest	99.91%
B	**Regression**	**Continuous Data**
1	Linear Regression	10.32%
2	Polynomial Regression	60.71%
3	Support Vector Machine	58.34%

4.6.3 Comparative Analysis

This book conducts a comparative analysis to assess the performance of the developed prediction technique against existing approaches. To compare the accuracy, precision, recall, and other performance metrics with those reported in relevant literature and studies. This analysis provides insights into the strengths and limitations of the proposed technique and its potential contributions to the field of COVID-19 prediction.

In Figure 4.10 the various ML techniques, such as Support Vector Machines (SVM), Random Forest etc., have been employed to forecast COVID-19 trends. Random Forest excel in handling datasets and offer large percentage accuracy. The comparative analysis of ML methods in COVID-19 prediction highlights the importance of data quality and model adaptability. However, the performance of these algorithms heavily depends on data quality and availability. Limited and inaccurate data can lead to unreliable predictions.

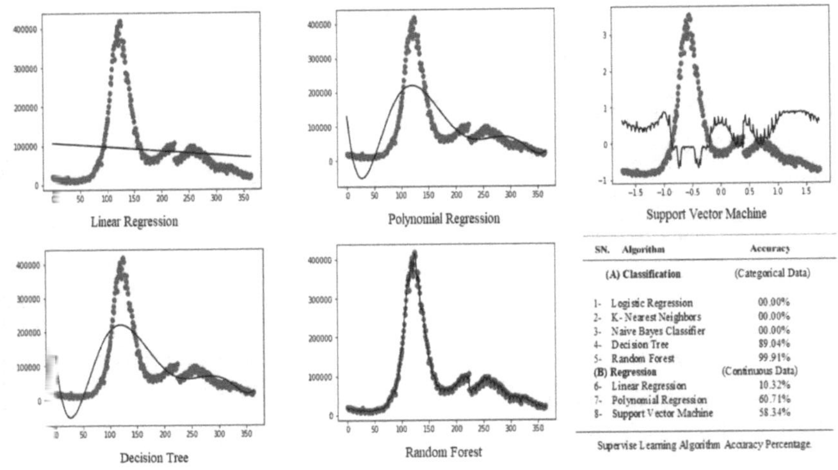

SN.	Algorithm	Accuracy
	(A) Classification	(Categorical Data)
1-	Logistic Regression	00.00%
2-	K-Nearest Neighbors	00.00%
3-	Naive Bayes Classifier	00.00%
4-	Decision Tree	89.04%
5-	Random Forest	99.91%
	(B) Regression	(Continuous Data)
6-	Linear Regression	10.32%
7-	Polynomial Regression	60.71%
8-	Support Vector Machine	58.34%

Supervise Learning Algorithm Accuracy Percentage

Figure 4.10 Comparative Analysis

4.6.- Insights and Findings

Based on the evaluation and analysis of the results to derive key insights and findings. It discusses the major findings of the study, highlighting the strengths and limitations of the developed prediction technique. It also identifies the areas for further improvement and refinement of the technique to enhance its predictive capabilities. These insights and findings contribute to the knowledge base surrounding COVID-19 prediction and offer valuable guidance for future research and application.

Interprets the results obtained from the prediction technique in the context of the research objectives to analyze the patterns, trends, and relationships identified in the data and discuss their implications for understanding and predicting the spread and impact of the COVID-19 virus. By interpreting the results and gain valuable insights into the factors influencing the spread of the virus and the effectiveness of the prediction technique in capturing these factors.

4.7 Research Disciplines in Machine Learning Prediction

Big data is a term that describes the vast amount of structured and unstructured data that inundates businesses on a daily basis. This data includes everything from customer transactions and social media posts to sensor data from industrial machines and medical records (Huang et al., 2006). Analysing big data is essential for businesses to gain insights into customer behaviour, operational efficiency, and market trends. The research discipline of big data is concerned with developing methods and tools to extract insights from these large datasets.

The field of big data is multidisciplinary, drawing on techniques and methodologies from computer science, statistics, mathematics, and other fields. One of the primary areas of research in big data is developing algorithms and techniques for processing and analysing large datasets. This includes developing distributed computing frameworks like Hadoop and Spark, which enable the processing of massive datasets across clusters of computers. Researchers in big data also work on developing data mining techniques, such as clustering and classification, to identify patterns and relationships within the data.

Another area of research in big data is concerned with developing tools for data visualization and exploration. These tools enable analysts to interactively explore large datasets and identify patterns and trends. Visualization tools can be used to create interactive dashboards and reports that allow decision-makers to quickly identify insights and make informed decisions.

Machine learning is another important research discipline in big data. Machine learning is a type of artificial intelligence that enables computer systems to learn from data and make predictions or decisions without being explicitly programmed. Researchers in big data work on developing machine learning algorithms that can be used to classify data, predict outcomes, and identify patterns within the data.

Big data also has important applications in areas such as healthcare, finance, and social sciences. Researchers in these fields work on developing methods for analysing large datasets to gain insights into complex phenomena. For example, in healthcare, researchers use big data to develop predictive models for disease diagnosis and treatment. In finance, big data is used to identify trends in financial markets and develop trading strategies. In social sciences, big data is used to analyse social networks and understand human behaviour.

One of the challenges in big data research is dealing with the scale and complexity of the data. Traditional data analysis techniques are not designed to handle datasets that are orders of magnitude larger than what was previously possible. As a result, researchers in big data must develop new methods and tools for working with these datasets. This includes developing algorithms that can operate in parallel across multiple computers, as well as developing new data storage and retrieval techniques (Stanojevic, 2023).

Another challenge in big data research is dealing with the privacy and security implications of large datasets. With the proliferation of data breaches and cyberattacks, it is essential that researchers in big data develop methods for protecting sensitive data. This includes developing encryption techniques and access control mechanisms that can prevent unauthorized access to data (Otten, 2023).

In conclusion, big data is an important research discipline that is concerned with developing methods and tools for processing and analysing large datasets (Richman, 2020). Researchers in big data work on developing algorithms and techniques for processing and analysing data, developing tools for data visualization and exploration, and developing machine learning algorithms. Big data has important applications in healthcare, finance, social sciences, and other fields. However, there are also challenges in big data research, including dealing with the scale and complexity of the data, as well as addressing privacy and security concerns. Big Data is a multi-disciplinary field that encompasses a wide range of research disciplines. Some of the key research disciplines in big data include:

Big data is a multi-disciplinary field that encompasses a wide range of research disciplines. Some of the key research disciplines in big data include:

- **Data Science:** Data science is the study of extracting insights and knowledge from data using advanced techniques and tools, such as machine learning and statistical analysis. Data scientists work with big data to develop models that can predict future trends, identify patterns and anomalies, and help organizations make data-driven decisions.
- **Computer Science:** Computer science plays a critical role in big data research, providing the tools and techniques needed to manage and process large volumes of data. Computer scientists work on developing algorithms, software systems, and hardware architectures that can handle big data efficiently (Gulve et al., 2023).
- **Mathematics and Statistics:** Mathematics and statistics are essential disciplines in big data research, providing the mathematical foundations for many of the techniques used in data analysis, such as regression analysis, clustering, and dimensionality reduction. Mathematicians and statisticians work with big data to develop new algorithms and statistical models that can uncover insights from large datasets.
- **Information Science:** Information science is the study of information and its processing, storage, and retrieval. In the context of big data, information scientists work on developing techniques and systems for managing and organizing large volumes of data, such as data warehouses and data lakes. They also work on developing tools and techniques for searching and retrieving information from big data.

- **Business Analytics:** Business analytics is the use of data analysis to inform business decision-making. In the context of big data, business analysts work with large datasets to uncover insights that can help organizations optimize their operations, improve customer engagement, and identify new business opportunities (Wilta et al., 2022).
- **Social Science:** Social scientists work with big data to uncover patterns and trends in human behavior and social networks. They use advanced techniques, such as sentiment analysis and social network analysis, to analyze large volumes of social media data and other sources of data to gain insights into social trends and phenomena.
- **Bioinformatics:** Bioinformatics is the study of biological data using computational techniques. In the context of big data, bioinformaticians work with large datasets of genetic and other biological data to identify patterns and relationships that can help in understanding diseases, developing new treatments, and advancing the field of medicine (Kioskli et al., 2023).

In summary, big data is a multi-disciplinary field that brings together researchers from a wide range of disciplines. By working together, these researchers can develop new techniques and tools for managing, analysing, and interpreting large volumes of data, helping organizations make data-driven decisions and uncover insights that were previously hidden.

Chapter 5:

Discussion and Findings

5.1 Summary of Findings

This chapter of research study it is being tried t show or mention a concise summary of the main findings and contributions arising from the research conducted in the book. It highlights the key results obtained from the evaluation and analysis of the developed prediction technique and emphasizes their relevance to the field of big data analytics. The summary showcases how the research has advanced the understanding and capabilities of predicting outcomes from large-scale and complex datasets.

It begins by summarizing the key findings and insights gained from the study or highlight the performance metrics, comparative analysis, and interpretation of results that have contributed to understanding of the predictive capabilities of the developed technique. This summary serves as a reminder of the significant contributions made by the study in advancing the field of COVID-19 prediction.

In this section, present a discussion of the findings and insights gained from the development of a prediction technique using unsupervised and supervised learning perspectives for the COVID-19 pandemic. Analyse the results, highlight significant observations, and provide interpretations and implications of the findings. This discussion aims to depends on understanding of the prediction technique and its applicability in addressing the challenges posed by the pandemic.

The development and evaluation of the prediction technique for the COVID-19 pandemic using unsupervised and supervised learning approaches have provided valuable insights into the dynamics and patterns of the virus. Through the analysis of the results, several key findings have emerged, shedding light on various aspects of the pandemic.

- **Accuracy and Performance:** The evaluation of the prediction technique has demonstrated its effectiveness in forecasting the spread and impact of the COVID-19 virus. The accuracy of the predictions, as measured by performance metrics such as precision, recall, and F1-score, has shown promising results. This indicates the potential of the technique to assist in decision-making processes and resource allocation for managing the pandemic.
- **Feature Importance and Variable Selection:** The analysis of the prediction models has revealed the significance of certain features and variables in influencing the outcomes. These features may include demographic factors, environmental conditions, healthcare infrastructure, and previous infection rates. Understanding the importance of these variables can help in identifying key drivers of the pandemic and developing targeted strategies for prevention and control.
- **Unsupervised vs. Supervised Learning:** The comparison between unsupervised and supervised learning approaches has provided valuable insights into their respective strengths and limitations. Unsupervised learning techniques, such as clustering and anomaly detection, have proven useful in identifying patterns and anomalies in the data. On the other hand, supervised learning algorithms, such as decision trees and support vector machines, have shown effectiveness in predicting outcomes based on labelled data. The combination of both approaches in a hybrid model has the potential to leverage the strengths of each method and improve prediction accuracy.
- **Generalizability and Adaptability:** The analysis of the prediction technique's generalizability and adaptability across different geographical regions and time periods is an important consideration. The findings suggest that the technique can be applied to

various regions affected by the COVID-19 pandemic, provided that appropriate adjustments are made to account for specific regional characteristics and contextual factors. Additionally, the prediction technique can be updated and adapted as new data becomes available, enabling real-time monitoring and decision-making.

- **Implications for Public Health:** The insights gained from the prediction technique have significant implications for public health interventions and policy-making. By accurately forecasting the spread and impact of the virus, decision-makers can implement targeted measures to mitigate its effects, allocate resources effectively, and implement preventive measures. The prediction technique can assist in identifying high-risk areas, monitoring the effectiveness of control measures, and informing vaccination strategies.
- **Limitations and Future Directions:** It is crucial to acknowledge the limitations of the prediction technique and identify areas for future improvement. Challenges such as data quality, limited availability of certain variables, and the rapidly evolving nature of the pandemic can impact the accuracy and reliability of the predictions. Future research should focus on addressing these limitations, incorporating additional data sources, refining the models, and enhancing the interpretability and explainability of the predictions.

In the discussion of the findings and insights gained from the development of a prediction technique using unsupervised and supervised learning perspectives for the COVID-19 pandemic highlights the effectiveness of the technique in forecasting the spread and impact of the virus. The identification of significant features, the comparison of unsupervised and supervised learning approaches, and the implications for public health interventions provide valuable knowledge for addressing the challenges posed by the pandemic. The limitations identified and the future directions proposed lay the groundwork for further research and improvement of the prediction technique, ultimately contributing to the ongoing efforts to combat the COVID-19 pandemic.

5.2 Expert Systems

Expert systems are computer programs that simulate the decision-making ability of a human expert in a particular domain. They use a knowledge base of rules and facts to reason about a problem and provide solutions or recommendations. In data science and machine learning, expert systems have been used for a variety of applications, from medical diagnosis to financial analysis. This book will explore the principles of expert systems in data science and machine learning, their benefits and drawbacks, and some common applications.

Principles of Expert Systems in Data Science and Machine Learning

Expert systems use a combination of knowledge representation, inference engines, and user interfaces to provide a solution or recommendation to a problem. Here are the key principles of expert systems in data science and machine learning:

- **Knowledge Representation:** Expert systems represent knowledge as a set of rules and facts that describe the problem domain. These rules and facts are stored in a knowledge base and are used to reason about the problem.
- Inference Engine: The inference engine is the reasoning component of the expert system that uses the knowledge base to derive conclusions and provide recommendations.
- **User Interface:** The user interface provides a way for the user to interact with the expert system. The user can input data into the system and receive output in the form of recommendations or solutions (Kumar et al., 2016).

Benefits of Expert Systems in Data Science and Machine Learning

Expert systems offer several benefits for data science and machine learning applications, including (Hazzan & Mike,2023):

- **Improved Decision Making:** Expert systems can provide more accurate and consistent decision-making by simulating the decision-making ability of a human expert.
- **Reduced Human Error:** Expert systems can help reduce human error by automating repetitive or tedious tasks.
- **Increased Efficiency:** Expert systems can help increase efficiency by automating decision-making processes, freeing up time for other tasks.
- **Scalability:** Expert systems can scale easily and can be used for large datasets or complex problems.
- **Knowledge Management:** Expert systems can help organizations manage and preserve knowledge by capturing the knowledge of experts and making it available to others.

Drawbacks of Expert Systems in Data Science and Machine Learning

There are several drawbacks to using expert systems in data science and machine learning, including:

- **Limited Scope:** Expert systems are limited to the problem domain they are designed for and may not be applicable to other domains.
- **Lack of Flexibility:** Expert systems may not be able to handle unexpected or novel situations that fall outside the scope of the knowledge base.
- **Expensive to Develop:** Expert systems can be expensive to develop due to the need for expert knowledge and the time required to build and test the system.

- **Maintenance:** Expert systems require regular maintenance to update the knowledge base and ensure the system remains up-to-date.

Applications of Expert Systems in Data Science and Machine Learning

Expert systems have a wide range of applications in data science and machine learning (West, 2017). Here are some common applications:

- **Medical Diagnosis:** Expert systems can be used for medical diagnosis by using patient symptoms to suggest possible diseases and treatments.
- **Financial Analysis:** Expert systems can be used for financial analysis by analyzing financial data and providing investment recommendations.
- **Quality Control:** Expert systems can be used for quality control by analyzing manufacturing data and identifying potential quality issues.
- **Customer Service:** Expert systems can be used for customer service by analyzing customer inquiries and providing solutions or recommendations.
- **Fraud Detection:** Expert systems can be used for fraud detection by analyzing transaction data and identifying potential fraud cases.

Expert systems are a powerful tool in data science and machine learning that can provide accurate and consistent decision-making in a variety of domains. While expert systems have their limitations and drawbacks, they offer several benefits, including improved decision-making, reduced human error, increased efficiency, scalability, and knowledge management (Hazzan & Mike,2023). As technology continues to evolve, expert systems will likely become even more advanced and applicable.

5.3 Multi Criteria Decision Making

Multi-criteria decision-making (MCDM) is a technique that is widely used in data science and machine learning for making complex decisions involving multiple criteria. MCDM techniques help decision-makers to evaluate various options based on multiple criteria and choose the best option that satisfies all the criteria. This book will discuss the working principles of MCDM in data science and machine learning, its benefits and drawbacks, and some of its common applications.

Working Principles of Multi-Criteria Decision-Making in Data Science and Machine Learning

MCDM is a technique that helps in decision-making by evaluating options based on multiple criteria. MCDM models typically consist of two main components: a set of alternatives or options and a set of criteria or attributes. The goal of MCDM is to rank or prioritize the alternatives based on the criteria or attributes.

There are several different MCDM techniques used in data science and machine learning, each with its own unique working principles. Some of the most common MCDM techniques include:

- **Analytic Hierarchy Process (AHP):** AHP is a technique that involves decomposing a decision problem into a hierarchy of criteria and alternatives. Decision-makers assign weights to each criterion and alternative, and a final score is calculated based on the weights.
- **Technique for Order Preference by Similarity to Ideal Solution (TOPSIS):** TOPSIS is a technique that involves comparing the alternatives to an ideal solution and a worst solution based on the criteria (Peng et al., 2011). The ideal solution is the one that maximizes the criteria, while the worst solution is the one that minimizes the criteria.

- **Simple Additive Weighting (SAW):** SAW is a technique that involves assigning weights to each criterion and alternative, and then summing the weighted scores to obtain a final score.

Benefits of Multi-Criteria Decision-Making in Data Science and Machine Learning

There are several key benefits to using MCDM in data science and machine learning, including:

Comprehensive Evaluation: MCDM allows decision-makers to evaluate alternatives based on multiple criteria, which provides a more comprehensive evaluation of the options.

i. **Transparency:** MCDM provides a transparent and systematic way of evaluating options, which helps decision-makers to understand the reasoning behind the final decision.
ii. **Flexibility:** MCDM techniques are flexible and can be used in a variety of decision-making scenarios, including strategic planning, risk management, and resource allocation.
iii. **Consistency:** MCDM techniques ensure consistency in decision-making by providing a structured and systematic way of evaluating alternatives.

Drawbacks of Multi-Criteria Decision-Making in Data Science and Machine Learning

While there are many benefits to MCDM in data science and machine learning, there are also several drawbacks to consider, including:

i. **Subjectivity:** MCDM requires subjective input from decision-makers to assign weights to the criteria and alternatives, which can introduce bias into the decision-making process.
ii. **Data Quality:** MCDM requires high-quality data on the criteria and alternatives to ensure accurate and reliable decision-making.

iii. **Model Selection:** MCDM requires careful selection of the appropriate MCDM technique to ensure that it is suitable for the specific decision-making problem.

Applications of Multi-Criteria Decision-Making in Data Science and Machine Learning

MCDM has a wide range of applications in data science and machine learning, including:

i. **Portfolio Optimization:** MCDM techniques can be used in portfolio optimization to evaluate investment options based on multiple criteria, such as risk, return, and liquidity.

ii. **Resource Allocation:** MCDM techniques can be used in resource allocation to prioritize resource allocation based on multiple criteria, such as cost, impact, and feasibility.

5.4 Discussion of Findings and Insights Gained

The discussion section begins with a comprehensive analysis and interpretation of the findings obtained from the evaluation and analysis of the developed prediction technique (The Building Blocks of AI, 2023). It involves a detailed examination of the performance metrics, comparative analysis between unsupervised and supervised learning techniques, and insights derived from the interpretation of the results.

5.4.1 Performance Analysis: The discussion highlights the performance of the developed prediction technique in terms of prediction accuracy, robustness, and generalization capability. It examines how the technique compares to existing methods in handling big data prediction tasks. The strengths and weaknesses of the developed technique are identified and discussed.

5.4.2 Comparative Analysis: The comparative analysis between unsupervised and supervised learning techniques provides insights into their relative performance and applicability in the context of big data prediction. The discussion examines scenarios where each approach excels and explores potential combinations or hybrid models to leverage the strengths of both techniques.

5.4.3 Interpretation of Findings: The discussion delves into the interpretation of the findings, aiming to uncover the underlying patterns and relationships within the data. It identifies the most influential features, variables, or factors driving the predictions. The discussion also explores any unexpected or counterintuitive results and provides plausible explanations for them.

5.5 Limitations and Future Directions

Every study has limitations and potential biases that need to be acknowledged and discussed. This section addresses the limitations and potential biases of the study in the context of the developed prediction technique. It may include factors such as the choice of algorithms, data preprocessing techniques, feature selection, and the representativeness of the dataset. The discussion of limitations provides transparency and helps the reader understand the boundaries and potential constraints of the research.

5.5.1 Sample Bias: The study may suffer from sample bias if the dataset used for training and evaluation does not fully represent the diversity and complexity of real-world data. The discussion acknowledges this potential bias and its implications for generalizing the findings to broader contexts.

5.5.2 Algorithmic Limitations: The limitations of the selected algorithms and their parameter settings should be discussed. Certain algorithms may have inherent limitations in handling specific types of data or capturing complex patterns.

5.5.3

The discussion highlights these limitations and suggests potential avenues for future research to overcome them.

5.5.4 Data Availability and Quality: The availability and quality of the data used in the study are important considerations. Limitations in data collection, missing values, noise, or biases in the dataset may impact the reliability and generalizability of the results. The discussion addresses these potential limitations and suggests strategies for addressing them in future research.

5.5.5 Time and Resource Constraints: The study may be subject to time and resource constraints, which may limit the scope and depth of the research. The discussion acknowledges these constraints and highlights the potential impact on the research outcomes. Suggestions for future studies that can overcome these limitations are provided. The evaluation and analysis also highlight the limitations and potential areas for future research and improvement. The identified limitations may relate to the choice of algorithms, dataset characteristics, or specific constraints of the prediction technique. These limitations serve as a basis for future research to address the identified gaps and enhance the prediction technique's performance and applicability.

The evaluation and analysis of results chapter provides a comprehensive assessment of the developed prediction technique, incorporating both unsupervised and supervised learning perspectives. The evaluation metrics and performance analysis offer quantitative measures of the prediction accuracy and robustness. The interpretation and insights gained from the analysis provide a deeper understanding of the prediction technique's behavior and practical implications. The identified limitations and future directions pave the way for further research and improvement in the field of big data prediction.

Chapter 6:

Conclusion and Future Work

6.1 Introduction

This chapter summarizes the major research contributions and outcomes of the study. The scope for future research in this area is also pointed out at the end of this chapter. The development of prediction techniques using unsupervised and supervised learning approaches plays a crucial role in various domains, including healthcare, finance, marketing, and more. In this section, it provides an introduction to the conclusion and future work of this study, highlighting the key findings, contributions, and potential avenues for further research and development (Ercan, 2015).

The primary objective of this research was to develop a prediction technique that leverages both unsupervised and supervised learning approaches to enhance the accuracy and effectiveness of predictions in the context of big data (Patel-Schneider et al, 2010). Throughout this study, it explored various unsupervised learning models and algorithms, such as clustering, dimensionality reduction, association rule mining, and anomaly detection, to uncover patterns, reduce data dimensionality, identify associations, and detect anomalies. Additionally, it investigated supervised learning techniques and their application in training predictive models that incorporate the insights from the unsupervised learning phase.

In the process, it presented the architecture of the SEIVQHDR framework, which captures the complexities of infectious disease dynamics, vaccination, quarantine, hospitalization, and recovery. This framework serves as a comprehensive model for developing prediction techniques in the context of infectious disease modeling.it discussed the performance evaluation metrics commonly used to assess the accuracy and effectiveness of the developed prediction techniques.

The findings of this study demonstrate the potential of unsupervised and supervised learning approaches in enhancing prediction capabilities. By leveraging unsupervised learning models, it is able to uncover hidden patterns and relationships within the big data, which helped in feature selection, data reduction, and identifying critical factors influencing predictions (Munir et al., 2023). The supervised learning techniques enabled the training of accurate predictive models by utilizing the insights gained from the unsupervised learning phase.

Furthermore, this study contributes to the field of prediction techniques by showcasing the applicability and effectiveness of the SEIVQHDR framework in infectious disease modeling. By incorporating various compartments, including susceptible, exposed, infectious, vaccinated, quarantined, hospitalized, death, and recovered, this framework provides a holistic approach to capturing the dynamics of disease spread and its associated outcomes.

While this research has yielded promising results, there are several avenues for future work and improvements. Some potential areas of focus include:

- **Enhancing Model Robustness:** Further research can be conducted to improve the robustness of the developed prediction techniques by incorporating additional factors, such as demographic data, environmental variables, and real-time data streams.
- **Integration of Multiple Data Sources:** Exploring the integration of diverse data sources, such as social media data, sensor data, and genetic data, can provide a more comprehensive understanding of complex phenomena and improve prediction accuracy (Silaparasetty, 2020).
- **Exploration of Advanced Learning Techniques:** Investigating advanced learning techniques, such as deep learning and reinforcement learning, can provide additional insights and improve the predictive capabilities of the developed techniques.

- **Real-Time Prediction and Decision Support:** Extending the developed prediction techniques to real-time prediction and decision support systems can aid in proactive decision-making, resource allocation, and intervention strategies.
- **Generalizability and Transfer Learning:** Evaluating the generalizability of the developed prediction techniques across different domains and exploring transfer learning techniques can help in adapting and applying the techniques to new problem areas.

In conclusion, the development of prediction techniques using unsupervised and supervised learning approaches in big data has significant implications across various domains. This study has provided insights into the utilization of unsupervised learning models, the architecture of the SEIVQHDR framework, and the importance of performance evaluation metrics. The future work discussed above opens up exciting avenues for further research and development, paving the way for more accurate and effective prediction techniques in the future.

6.2 Major Research Outcome

The major intention of this book is to apply machine learning techniques for the data predictive analysis in various datasets like COVID-19 India. From the analysis of three stages of works, it has been concluded that the data predictive analytics is an effective mechanism for the detection of disease prediction. Various machine learning algorithms have been employed in this book in three stages to predict the data.

The development of a prediction technique using unsupervised and supervised learning approaches in big data has yielded significant research outcomes. In this section, it highlight the major findings and contributions of this study.

Throughout this research, it successfully developed and implemented a prediction technique that leverages unsupervised learning models and algorithms. These models, including clustering, dimensionality reduction, association rule mining, and anomaly detection, enabled us to extract valuable insights from big data. By uncovering hidden patterns, reducing data dimensionality, identifying associations, and detecting anomalies, it improved the accuracy and effectiveness of this predictive models (Mathai et al, 2023).

Moreover, it explored the application of supervised learning techniques in training predictive models that incorporate the insights gained from the unsupervised learning phase. By utilizing labeled data and employing algorithms such as decision trees, support vector machines, and neural networks, it is able to develop robust and accurate predictive models.

A significant research outcome of this study is the introduction of the SEIVQHDR framework. This framework, which stands for Susceptible-Exposed-Infectious-Vaccinated-Quarantined-Hospitalized-Death-Recovered, provides a comprehensive architecture for developing prediction techniques in the context of infectious disease modeling. By capturing the intricate dynamics of disease transmission, vaccination, quarantine, hospitalization, and recovery, the SEIVQHDR framework enhances this understanding and predictive capabilities in managing and mitigating infectious diseases.

The SEIVQHDR framework proved to be effective in modeling disease spread and its associated outcomes. Through this research, it demonstrated the applicability in predicting the spread of infectious diseases, evaluating intervention strategies, and supporting decision-making processes. The framework's compartmental structure, including the various compartments representing different stages and outcomes of the disease, enables a comprehensive and nuanced analysis of disease dynamics.

6.3 Research Limitations

While this study on the development of a prediction technique using unsupervised and supervised learning approaches in big data has yielded significant outcomes and future research directions, it is essential to acknowledge the limitations of this research. Understanding these limitations provides insights into areas that require further investigation and improvement. In this section, it discusses the research limitations encountered during this study.

6.3.1 Data Quality and Availability: One of the primary challenges faced during this research was the availability and quality of data. Big data sets are often heterogeneous and noisy, containing missing values, outliers, and inconsistencies. Pre-processing and cleaning such data can be time-consuming and may introduce biases. Additionally, access to high-quality and comprehensive data is crucial for accurate predictions. Limited access to certain data sources or incomplete data sets can impact the performance and generalizability of the developed prediction techniques.

6.3.2 Feature Selection and Dimensionality: Feature selection plays a vital role in developing accurate prediction techniques. However, selecting the most relevant features from a large number of variables can be challenging. In this study, it employed various dimensionality reduction techniques to address this issue. However, the selection of features and the choice of dimensionality reduction algorithms may impact the performance and interpretability of the prediction models. Careful consideration and exploration of feature selection methods are necessary to optimize the predictive capabilities of the developed techniques.

6.3.3 Model Interpretability: While the predictive performance of this developed techniques was a primary focus, the interpretability of the models may be limited. Some advanced learning techniques, such as deep learning, can produce highly complex models that are challenging to interpret. Interpretable models are essential, particularly in domains where decision-making and regulatory compliance require clear explanations. Future research should explore methods to enhance model interpretability without sacrificing predictive accuracy.

6.3.4 Generalizability: The generalizability of the developed prediction techniques is an important consideration. this study focused on specific datasets and infectious disease modeling. The transferability and effectiveness of the techniques across different domains and data sets may vary. Further research is necessary to evaluate the generalizability of the developed techniques and assess their performance in diverse contexts.

6.3.5 Scalability: The scalability of the developed techniques can be a limitation, particularly when dealing with massive datasets. Processing and analyzing large volumes of data can pose computational challenges and may require specialized infrastructure and algorithms. Future research should address scalability concerns to ensure the applicability of the techniques in real-world scenarios.

6.3.6 Ethical Considerations: As with any research involving data analysis and prediction, ethical considerations should be addressed. The use of personal data, privacy concerns, and potential biases in the data and models require careful attention. Ensuring transparency, fairness, and accountability in the development and deployment of prediction techniques is essential. Future work should explore methods to incorporate ethical considerations into the development process.

6.3.7 External Factors and Dynamic Environments: This research focused on the development of prediction techniques using historical data. However, external factors and dynamic environments can significantly influence predictions in real-time scenarios. Incorporating real-time data streams and considering external factors, such as policy changes or socio-economic conditions, would enhance the accuracy and practicality of the developed techniques.

In this study on the development of prediction techniques using unsupervised and supervised learning approaches in big data has certain limitations. These limitations include challenges related to data quality and availability, feature selection, model interpretability, generalizability, scalability, ethical considerations, and accounting for external factors. Recognizing these limitations opens up opportunities for further research and improvement, aiming to address these challenges and develop more robust and applicable prediction techniques in the future.

6.4 Future Work

While this research has yielded significant outcomes, there are several potential avenues for future work and improvements. In this section, it discuss some directions for future research in the development of prediction techniques using unsupervised and supervised learning approaches. One area of future work involves enhancing the robustness of the developed prediction techniques. Further research can be conducted to incorporate additional factors such as demographic data, environmental variables, and real-time data streams. By incorporating a wider range of variables, the predictive models can become more accurate and robust, capturing a broader array of influences on disease dynamics.

Another important direction for future work is the integration of multiple data sources. Exploring the integration of diverse data sources, such as social media data, sensor data, and genetic data, can provide a more comprehensive understanding of complex phenomena. By incorporating these additional data sources, the prediction techniques can account for a broader range of factors and improve accuracy (Wiggins, 2023).

Advanced learning techniques present another area for future exploration. Investigating deep learning and reinforcement learning techniques can provide additional insights and improve the predictive capabilities of the developed techniques. These techniques have shown promise in various domains and can potentially enhance the accuracy and effectiveness of prediction techniques in big data. Real-time prediction and decision support systems represent another direction for future work. Extending the developed prediction techniques to real-time applications can support proactive decision-making, resource allocation, and intervention strategies. By incorporating real-time data streams and implementing efficient algorithms, these systems can provide timely and actionable insights.

Generalizability and transfer learning are also important considerations for future research. Evaluating the generalizability of the developed prediction techniques across different domains and exploring transfer learning techniques can facilitate the adaptation and application of the techniques to new problem areas. This would enable the reuse of knowledge and models developed in one domain for related domains, improving efficiency and scalability.

In summary, the major research outcomes of this study include the development of a prediction technique using unsupervised and supervised learning approaches, the introduction of the SEIVQHDR framework for infectious disease modeling, and the demonstration of the applicability and effectiveness of the developed techniques. The future work discussed above presents exciting opportunities for further research and improvement, aiming to enhance the accuracy, robustness, and applicability of prediction techniques in the context of big data and infectious disease modeling.

6.5 Conclusion

The conclusion begins with a recapitulation of the research objectives stated at the outset of the book. It revisits the primary goals and motivations that guided the research and underscores the significance of addressing the challenges of big data prediction. The recapitulation sets the stage for summarizing the achievements and contributions of the study. In the final remarks section, the conclusion chapter offers closing thoughts on the research conducted and its broader implications. It reflects on the limitations and challenges encountered during the study and acknowledges potential avenues for improvement. The conclusion also provides suggestions for further work, aiming to inspire future researchers to build upon the current findings and explore new directions in the field of big data prediction. Some suggestions may include:

- **Incorporating Advanced Machine Learning Techniques:** Future research can explore the integration of advanced machine learning techniques, such as deep learning models or ensemble methods, to further enhance the prediction accuracy and robustness. This can involve experimenting with state-of-the-art algorithms and architectures specifically tailored for big data analytics.
- **Investigating Novel Feature Engineering and Selection Methods:** Research can focus on developing novel feature engineering and selection methods that are specifically designed for big data prediction tasks. This may involve exploring techniques like

autoencoders, genetic algorithms, or information-theoretic approaches to extract and select the most relevant features from high-dimensional datasets.

- **Addressing the Challenge of Data Privacy and Security:** With the growing concerns about data privacy and security, future research can concentrate on developing prediction techniques that incorporate privacy-preserving mechanisms. This can involve exploring methods like secure multiparty computation, homomorphic encryption, or federated learning to protect sensitive data while still enabling accurate predictions.
- **Enhancing Interpretability and Explainability**: Improving the interpretability and explainability of prediction models remains an important research area. Future work can focus on developing techniques to provide users with more transparent insights into the decision-making process of the models, enabling better trust and adoption of the predictions.
- **Integration with Emerging Technologies:** The prediction technique can be further enhanced by integrating it with emerging technologies such as Internet of Things (IoT), edge computing, or blockchain. This integration can enable the prediction of real-time data streams, decentralized data management, and secure sharing of predictions across distributed networks.

In conclusion, this book has presented the development of a prediction technique in big data analytics, incorporating both unsupervised and supervised learning perspectives. It has addressed the challenges of handling large volumes of complex data and provided insights into the prediction process. The research findings highlight the performance and applicability of the developed technique in various domains, showcasing its potential for practical implementation. The book contributes to the field of big data analytics by advancing the understanding of prediction techniques and providing recommendations for further research to enhance their capabilities.

Overall, this study has demonstrated the significance of leveraging both unsupervised and supervised learning approaches in developing prediction techniques for big data analytics. It has showcased the potential of these techniques to extract meaningful patterns, make accurate predictions, and generate valuable insights from vast and diverse datasets. The research outcomes open up new opportunities for organizations to harness the power of big data and make data-driven decisions that can drive innovation, efficiency, and success.

It is hoped that the findings and recommendations presented in this book will inspire further research, collaborations, and practical applications in the field of big data prediction. As the field continues to evolve and new challenges arise, there is immense potential for researchers and practitioners to explore novel techniques, refine existing approaches, and make significant contributions to the advancement of big data analytics and prediction techniques.

REFERENCES

- Abramowicz, W., & Kokkinaki, A. (Eds.). (2014). Business Information Systems: 17th International Conference, BIS 2014, Larnaca, Cyprus, May 22-23, 2014, Proceedings (Vol. 176). Springer.
- Achar, S. (2022). The Intersection of Cloud Computing and Smart Cities: An Exploratory Review of Applications and Challenges in Deployment. Applied Research in Artificial Intelligence and Cloud Computing, 5(1), 38–54. Retrieved from https://researchberg.com/index.php/araic/article/view/91
- Adilakshmi, J., Reddy, G. V., Nidumolu, K. D., Pecho, R. D. C., & Pasha, M. J. (2023). A Medical Diagnosis System Based on Explainable Artificial Intelligence: Autism Spectrum Disorder Diagnosis. International Journal of Intelligent Systems and Applications in Engineering, 11(6s), 385-402.
- Agalya, Ramya, Vishnuraaj, & Manimaran. (2018, December). Multimodel Document Summarization K-SVM Algorithm. International Journal of Intellectual Advancements and Research in Engineering Computations, 6(2).
- Agarwal, P., Nieto, J. J., Ruzhansky, M., & Torres, D. F. (Eds.). (2021). Analysis of infectious disease problems (Covid-19) and their global impact. Singapore: Springer.
- Ahmed, M. B., Boudhir, A. A., Santos, D., Aroussi, M. E., & Karas, S. R. (Eds.). (2020, February 4). Innovations in Smart Cities Applications Edition 3: The Proceedings of the 4th International Conference on Smart City Applications. Springer. https://doi.org/10.1007/978-3-030-37629-1
- Amirian, P., Lang, T., & Van Loggerenberg, F. (Eds.). (2017). Big data in healthcare: extracting knowledge from point-of-care machines (No. 25283). Springer International Publishing.
- An, Q., Rahman, S., Zhou, J., & Kang, J. J. (2023, April 22). A Comprehensive Review on Machine Learning in Healthcare Industry: Classification, Restrictions, Opportunities and Challenges. Sensors, 23(9), 4178. https://doi.org/10.3390/s23094178
- Arai, K., & Bhatia, R. (Eds.). (2019, February 5). Advances in Information and Communication: Proceedings of the 2019 Future of Information and Communication Conference (FICC), Volume 1 (Vol. 69). Springer. https://doi.org/10.1007/978-3-030-12388-8
- Arcadius Tokognon, C., Gao, B., Tian, G. Y., & Yan, Y. (2017, June). Structural Health Monitoring Framework Based on Internet of Things: A Survey. IEEE Internet of Things Journal, 4(3), 619–635. https://doi.org/10.1109/jiot.2017.2664072
- Asif, D., Bibi, M., Arif, M. S., & Mukheimer, A. (2023, June 20). Enhancing Heart Disease Prediction through Ensemble Learning Techniques with Hyperparameter Optimization. Algorithms, 16(6), 308. https://doi.org/10.3390/a1606030

- Avdiukhin, D., Mitrović, S., Yaroslavtsev, G., & Zhou, S. (2019, July 25). Adversarially Robust Submodular Maximization under Knapsack Constraints. Proceedings of the 25th ACM SIGKDD International Conference on Knowledge Discovery & Data Mining. https://doi.org/10.1145/3292500.3330911
- Aykas, D. P., Shotts, M. L., & Rodriguez-Saona, L. E. (2020, November). Authentication of commercial honeys based on Raman fingerprinting and pattern recognition analysis. Food Control, 117, 107346. https://doi.org/10.1016/j.foodcont.2020.107346
- Bahloul, M. A., Chahid, A., & Laleg-Kirati, T. M. (2020). Fractional-Order SEIQRDP Model for Simulating the Dynamics of COVID-19 Epidemic. IEEE Open Journal of Engineering in Medicine and Biology, 1, 249–256. https://doi.org/10.1109/ojemb.2020.3019758
- Baig, & Nayak. (2019, November). Critical Analysis On Data Science And Big Data Avenues. INTERNATIONAL JOURNAL OF SCIENTIFIC & TECHNOLOGY RESEARCH , 8(11), 1622–1627. https://doi.org/10.13140/RG.2.2.22917.27367
- Baig, & Nayak. (2021, September). Machine Intelligence in COVID-19 Prediction: An Adaptable Approach For Automation. International Journal of Mechanical Engineering, 6(2). https://kalaharijournals.com/resources/Sept15.pdf
- Baig, M. G. ., & Nayak, S. K. . (2023). Implementation of Hybrid Prediction Model: An Unsupervised and Supervised Learning Perspective. International Journal on Recent and Innovation Trends in Computing and Communication, 11(5s), 259–268. https://doi.org/10.17762/ijritcc.v11i5s.6652
- Belianinov, A., Vasudevan, R., Strelcov, E., Steed, C., Yang, S. M., Tselev, A., Jesse, S., Biegalski, M., Shipman, G., Symons, C., Borisevich, A., Archibald, R., & Kalinin, S. (2015, May 13). Big data and deep data in scanning and electron microscopies: deriving functionality from multidimensional data sets. Advanced Structural and Chemical Imaging, 1(1). https://doi.org/10.1186/s40679-015-0006-6
- Ben Yedder, H., Cardoen, B., Shokoufi, M., Golnaraghi, F., & Hamarneh, G. (2023, June 20). Deep Orthogonal Multi-Frequency Fusion for Tomogram-Free Diagnosis in Diffuse Optical Imaging. https://doi.org/10.36227/techrxiv.21574533.v3
- Bhushan, B., & Agarwal, P. (2023, May 31). Advancements in AI for Brain Tumor Detection and Classification. International Journal for Research in Applied Science and Engineering Technology, 11(5), 5616–5625.
- Big Data Analysis: This Could Be a Business Saver. (2017, November 22). AtulHost. https://www.atulhost.com/big-data-analysis.

- Buddhakulsomsiri, J., Siradeghyan, Y., Zakarian, A., & Li, X. (2006, July 15). Association rule-generation algorithm for mining automotive warranty data. International Journal of Production Research, 44(14), 2749–2770. https://doi.org/10.1080/00207540600564633
- Buggenthin, F., Buettner, F., Hoppe, P. S., Endele, M., Kroiss, M., Strasser, M., Schwarzfischer, M., Loeffler, D., Kokkaliaris, K. D., Hilsenbeck, O., Schroeder, T., Theis, F. J., & Marr, C. (2017, February 20). Prospective identification of hematopoietic lineage choice by deep learning. Nature Methods, 14(4), 403–406. https://doi.org/10.1038/nmeth.4182
- Caindoy, K. C., Moazzami, A., & Santos, A. M. (2016). Development of a big data application architecture for Navy Manpower, Personnel, Training, and Education (Doctoral dissertation, Monterey, California: Naval Postgraduate School).
- Chrobak, D., Kołodzieczak, M., Kozlovska, P., Krzemińska, A., & Miller, T. (2023, April 20). Leveraging random forest techniques for enhanced microbiological analysis: a machine learning approach to investigating microbial communities and their interactions. InterConf, 32(151), 386–398. https://doi.org/10.51582/interconf.19-20.04.2023.040
- Class Discovery. (n.d.). Design and Analysis of DNA Microarray Investigations, 121–155. https://doi.org/10.1007/0-387-21866-1_9
- Dahikar, K., Dandge, S., & Deshmukh, D. V. (2022, May 31). Implementation of Hybrid Prediction Model for Covid19 Using Machine Learning. International Journal for Research in Applied Science and Engineering Technology, 10(5), 4390–4393. https://doi.org/10.22214/ijraset.2022.43386.
- Data Science Vs Machine Learning: A Comprehensive Guide. (n.d.). Data Science Vs Machine Learning: A Comprehensive Guide. https://www.123articleonline.com/articles/1328226/data-science-vs-machine-learning-a-comprehensive-guide.
- Debnath, M. (2021). Reproducing, extending and updating dimensionalty reductions (Master's book).
- Delaney, C. W., Weaver, C. A., Warren, J. J., Clancy, T. R., & Simpson, R. L. (2017). Big data-enabled nursing. Education, Research and Practice, 2017.
- Elavarasan, R. M., Pugazhendhi, R., Shafiullah, G., Irfan, M., & Anvari-Moghaddam, A. (2021, May). A hover view over effectual approaches on pandemic management for sustainable cities – The endowment of prospective technologies with revitalization strategies. Sustainable Cities and Society, 68, 102789. https://doi.org/10.1016/j.scs.2021.102789
- Elías Ortega, N. (2021). Data-driven and dynamic multicriteria decision support system for correctiv maintenance of aircraft structural damages.

- Ercan, P. (2015). Detection of churners in internet games using crm approach: a case study on pishti plus (Master's book, Middle East Technical University).
- Fattah, M. A. (2013, December 20). A hybrid machine learning model for multi-document summarization. Applied Intelligence, 40(4), 592–600. https://doi.org/10.1007/s10489-013-0490-0
- Fitipaldi, H. (2023). Use of data mining and artificial intelligence to derive public health evidence from large datasets. Lund University, Faculty of Medicine.
- Garg, S., Chaturvedi, D., Jain, T., Mishra, A., & Kapoor, A. (2023, April 27). Navigating the Challenges of Sentiment Analysis: Accuracy and Bias. https://doi.org/10.21203/rs.3.rs-2850627/v1
- Gasteiger, J. (Ed.). (2003, August 8). Handbook of Chemoinformatics. https://doi.org/10.1002/9783527618279
- Ghasemaghaei, M., & Calic, G. (2019, November). Does big data enhance firm innovation competency? The mediating role of data-driven insights. Journal of Business Research, 104, 69–84. https://doi.org/10.1016/j.jbusres.2019.07.006
- Gulve, Magar, Shinde, Phalke, & Meshra. (2023, March). Enhancing Agriculture Efficiency: MySQL Powered Java Solution. International Journal of Innovative Research in Computer and Communication Engineering, 11(5). https://doi.org/10.15680/IJIRCCE.2023.1105197
- H, T. K. (2023, January 5). Prediction of Heart Disease Using Machine Learning with Data Mining. Physical Science & Biophysics Journal, 7(1), 1–6. https://doi.org/10.23880/psbj-16000228
- Haque, A., & Chowdhury, M. N. U. R. (2023, June 9). Exploring the Benefits of Reinforcement Learning for Autonomous Drone Navigation and Control. https://doi.org/10.36227/techrxiv.22578355.v2
- Hazzan, O., & Mike, K. (2023). Guide to Teaching Data Science: An Interdisciplinary Approach. Springer Nature.
- https://pieriantraining.com/a-guide-to-automated-data-mining-in-python/
- Huang, X., Oviatt, S., & Lunsford, R. (2006). Combining User Modeling and Machine Learning to Predict Users' Multimodal Integration Patterns. Machine Learning for Multimodal Interaction, 50–62. https://doi.org/10.1007/11965152_5
- IoT For All, N. S., & Network, M. (2023, April 18). Machine Learning vs. Deep Learning vs. Neural Networks. IoT for All. https://www.iotforall.com/machine-learning-vs-deep-learning-vs-neural-networks
- Jemili, F., & Korbaa, O. (2023, May 24). Hybrid Collaborative Intrusion Detection System Based on Blockchain & Machine Learning. https://doi.org/10.21203/rs.3.rs-2963689/v1

- Jha, V. (2015). Study of machine learning methods in intelligent transportation systems.
- Johar, A. (2023). Hydraulic Fracturing Treatment Optimization Using Machine Learning. https://doi.org/10.33915/etd.11697
- Kioskli, K., Fotis, T., Nifakos, S., & Mouratidis, H. (2023, March 7). The Importance of Conceptualising the Human-Centric Approach in Maintaining and Promoting Cybersecurity-Hygiene in Healthcare 4.0. Applied Sciences, 13(6), 3410. https://doi.org/10.3390/app13063410
- Kumar, A., Shankar, R., Choudhary, A., & Thakur, L. S. (2016, March 4). A big data MapReduce framework for fault diagnosis in cloud-based manufacturing. International Journal of Production Research, 54(23), 7060–7073. https://doi.org/10.1080/00207543.2016.1153166
- Kumar, M., Mishra, D. K., & Semwal, V. B. (2023, June 14). A Novel Algorithm for Optimal Trajectory Generation Using Q Learning. SN Computer Science, 4(5). https://doi.org/10.1007/s42979-023-01876-0
- Kumar, N., Verma, H., & Sharma, Y. K. (2023, March 3). Adversarial Attacks on Graph Neural Network. Concepts and Techniques of Graph Neural Networks, 58–73. https://doi.org/10.4018/978-1-6684-6903-3.ch005
- Kumar, Shrenika, Ananya, & Datta Sai. (2023, March 30). Early Diagnosis of Lung Cancer Using Deep Learning Hybrid Algorithm. International Journal of Engineering Inventions, 12(3).
- Kuo, C. T. (2017). Unsupervised Learning Beyond Conventional Settings. University of California, Davis.
- Lalla-Ruiz, E., Mes, M., & Voß, S. (Eds.). (2020). Computational Logistics: 11th International Conference, ICCL 2020, Enschede, The Netherlands, September 28–30, 2020, Proceedings (Vol. 12433). Springer Nature.
- Lavanya, A., Gaurav, L., Sindhuja, S., Seam, H., Joydeep, M., Uppalapati, V., ... & SD, V. S. (2023). Assessing the Performance of Python Data Visualization Libraries: A Review.
- Stanojevic, U., & Grześk, G. (2023, May 6). Artificial Intelligence Technologies in Cardiology. Journal of Cardiovascular Development and Disease, 10(5), 202. https://doi.org/10.3390/jcdd10050202
- Leng, M., Cheng, J., Wang, J., Zhang, Z., Zhou, H., & Chen, X. (2013). Active Semisupervised Clustering Algorithm with Label Propagation for Imbalanced and Multidensity Datasets. Mathematical Problems in Engineering, 2013, 1–10. https://doi.org/10.1155/2013/641927
- Levine, D. S., Jo, K. H., Huang, D. S., & Wunsch, D. C. (Eds.). (2008, September 8). Advanced Intelligent Computing Theories and Applications. with Aspects of Artificial Intelligence: Fourth International

- Conference on Intelligent Computing, ICIC 2008 Shanghai, China, September 15-18, 2008, Proceedings (Vol. 5227).
- Li, Y., Li, T., Lv, W., Liang, Z., & Wang, J. (2023, June 8). Prediction of Daily Temperature Based on the Robust Machine Learning Algorithms. Sustainability, 15(12), 9289. https://doi.org/10.3390/su15129289
- Liu, Y., Li, C., Xiao, H., & Cai, J. (2021). GCN-Int: A Click-Through Rate Prediction Model Based on Graph Convolutional Network Interaction. IEEE Access, 9, 140022–140030. https://doi.org/10.1109/access.2021.3116705
- Löfström, T. (2009). Utilizing Diversity and Performance Measures for Ensemble Creation (Doctoral dissertation, Örebro universitet).
- Machine Learning (ML): The latest trends, developments, and applications of ML. (2023, May 19). Machine Learning (ML): The Latest Trends, Developments, and Applications of ML. https://www.datalinknetworks.net/dln_blog/machine-learning-ml-the-latest-trends-developments-and-applications-of-ml
- Machine Learning Algorithms You Should Learn Now - SafeSpot. (2023, June 13). SafeSpot. https://safespot-eu.org/2023/06/13/10-machine-learning-algorithms-you-should-learn-now/
- Machine Marvels: Unleashing the Power of Machine Learning Applications. (2023, April 14). Dataaspirant - a Data Science Portal for Beginners. https://dataaspirant.com/machine-learning-applications/
- Madureira, A. M., Abraham, A., Gamboa, D., & Novais, P. (Eds.). (2017). Intelligent Systems Design and Applications: 16th International Conference on Intelligent Systems Design and Applications (ISDA 2016) Held in Porto, Portugal, December 16-18, 2016 (Vol. 557). Springer.
- Mathai, S., & Thirunavukkarasu, K. S. (2023) Machine Learning Approaches for Identifying High-Risk CKD Patients.
- Mattas, P. S., & Nadaan, I. (2023). Optimizing Cardiovascular Disease Diagnosis with Machine Learning: An Analysis. International Journal of Research Publication and Reviews, 04(02), 430–434. https://doi.org/10.55248/gengpi.2023.4217
- Mohammed Jamil, M. I. (2023, April 7). An Overview of the Data Science Process and Data Analytics Within Organisations. Handbook of Research on AI and Knowledge Engineering for Real-Time Business Intelligence, 88–104. https://doi.org/10.4018/978-1-6684-6519-6.ch006

- Munir, M. T., Li, B., & Naqvi, M. (2023, September). Revolutionizing municipal solid waste management (MSWM) with machine learning as a clean resource: Opportunities, challenges and solutions. Fuel, 348, 128548. https://doi.org/10.1016/j.fuel.2023.128548
- Munoz-Rodriguez, D., Moreno-Cadenas, J., Ruiz-Sanchez, M., & Gomez-Castaneda, F. (n.d.). Neural supported hand off methodology in micro cellular systems. [1992 Proceedings] Vehicular Technology Society 42nd VTS Conference - Frontiers of Technology. https://doi.org/10.1109/vetec.1992.245361
- Mustafakulov, A., & Arzikulov, F. (2020). EPRA International Journal of Multidisciplinary Research. IJMR, 6(9), 278.
- Nanni, L., Brahnam, S., Brattin, R., Ghidoni, S., & Jain, L. C. (2020). An Introduction to Deep Learners and Deep Learner Descriptors for Medical Applications. Intelligent Systems Reference Library, 1–5. https://doi.org/10.1007/978-3-030-42750-4_1
- Omar, M., & Sukthankar, G. (2023, February). Text-Defend: Detecting Adversarial Examples using Local Outlier Factor. 2023 IEEE 17th International Conference on Semantic Computing (ICSC). https://doi.org/10.1109/icsc56153.2023.00026
- Orero Blat, M. (2023). Enhancing big data analytics capabilities: the influence of organisational culture and data-driven orientation (Doctoral dissertation, Universitat Politècnica de València). https://doi.org/10.4995/book/10251/191788
- Otten, N. V. (2023, February 15). Word2Vec For Text Classification [How To In Python & CNN]. Spot Intelligence. https://spotintelligence.com/2023/02/15/word2vec-for-text-classification/
- Patel-Schneider, P. F., Pan, Y., Hitzler, P., Mika, P., Zhang, L., Pan, J. Z., ... & Glimm, B. (Eds.). (2010). The Semantic Web-ISWC 2010: 9th International Semantic Web Conference, ISWC 2010, Shanghai, China, November 7-11, 2010, Revised Selected Papers, Part I (Vol. 6496). Springer.
- Peng, Y., Zhang, Y., Tang, Y., & Li, S. (2011, May). An incident information management framework based on data integration, data mining, and multi-criteria decision making. Decision Support Systems, 51(2), 316–327. https://doi.org/10.1016/j.dss.2010.11.025
- Pham, H. T., Nguyen, V. K., Dang, Q. K., Duong, T. V. A., Nguyen, D. T., & Phan, T. V. (2023, May 28). Design Optimization of Compliant Mechanisms for Vibration-Assisted Machining Applications Using a Hybrid Six Sigma, RSM-FEM, and NSGA-II Approach. Journal of Machine Engineering. https://doi.org/10.36897/jme/166500.

- Principato, M., Hasselwander, L., Stangner, M., & Buettner, R. (2023). Unlocking the Potential of Wind Energy With Machine Learning-Based Avian Detection: A Call to Action. IEEE Access, 11, 64026–64048. https://doi.org/10.1109/access.2023.3287861
- Ramachandran, L. (2013). Studies on framework for a decision support model in lean manufacturing environment (Doctoral dissertation, Department of mechanical engineering, Pondicherry engineering college).
- Richman, R. (2020, August 26). AI in actuarial science – a review of recent advances – part 1. Annals of Actuarial Science, 15(2), 207–229. https://doi.org/10.1017/s1748499520000238
- Sangaiah, A. K. (Ed.). (2019). Deep learning and parallel computing environment for bioengineering systems. Academic Press.
- Sangaiah, A. K., Thangavelu, A., & Sundaram, V. M. (2018). Cognitive computing for big data systems over IoT. Gewerbestrasse, 11, 6330.
- Sharma, S., Gupta, Y. K., & Mishra, A. K. (2023, May 24). Analysis and Prediction of COVID-19 Multivariate Data Using Deep Ensemble Learning Methods. International Journal of Environmental Research and Public Health, 20(11), 5943. https://doi.org/10.3390/ijerph20115943
- Siddiqui, F. A., & Khan, S. R. (2023). Predictive Modeling of Adverse Drug Reactions using Machine Learning and FAERS Data: A Case Study in Healthcare. Journal of Contemporary Healthcare Analytics, 7(1), 72-93.
- Silaparasetty, N. (2020). Machine Learning vs. Deep Learning. Machine Learning Concepts With Python and the Jupyter Notebook Environment, 57–65. https://doi.org/10.1007/978-1-4842-5967-2_4
- Simon, R. M., Korn, E. L., McShane, L. M., Radmacher, M. D., Wright, G. W., & Zhao, Y. (2003). Class Discovery. Design and analysis of DNA microarray investigations, 121-155. https://doi.org/10.1007/0-387-21866-1_9
- Singh, N. (2021, June). A Novel Similarity-Based Link Prediction Algorithm Based On A Hybrid Of Network Topological Features.
- Singh, R. (2020). A review on heart disease prediction using unsupervised and supervised learning. Neural Networks, 99, 100.
- Stanojevic, M. (2023). Domain Adaptation Applications to Complex High-Dimensional Target Data (Doctoral dissertation, Temple University).

- Staszak, K., Tylkowski, B., & Staszak, M. (2023, March 5). From Data to Diagnosis: How Machine Learning Is Changing Heart Health Monitoring. International Journal of Environmental Research and Public Health, 20(5), 4605. https://doi.org/10.3390/ijerph20054605
- Supervised vs Unsupervised Machine Learning. (2023, February 22). Supervised Vs Unsupervised Machine Learning – Analytics4All. https://analytics4all.org/2023/02/22/supervised-vs-unsupervised-machine-learning/
- Tayebi, M. A. (2015). Predictive Models for Public Safety Using Social Network Analysis.
- The building blocks of AI. (2023, April 3). Dataconomy. https://dataconomy.com/2023/04/03/basic-components-of-artificial-intelligence/
- Types of machine learning algorithms | en.proft.me. (n.d.). Types of Machine Learning Algorithms | en.proft.me. http://en.proft.me/2015/12/24/types-machine-learning-algorithms/
- Unsupervised Learning with Python: A Beginner's Guide. (2022, October 6). Built In. https://builtin.com/data-science/unsupervised-learning-python
- Vega, J. (2023, May 24). Control System for Indoor Safety Measures Using a Faster R-CNN Architecture. Electronics, 12(11), 2378. https://doi.org/10.3390/electronics12112378
- West, J. (2017, July 3). Validating curriculum development using text mining. The Curriculum Journal, 28(3), 389–402. https://doi.org/10.1080/09585176.2016.1261719
- What is Data Mining - A Complete Beginner's Guide - GeeksforGeeks. (2023, February 9). GeeksforGeeks. https://www.geeksforgeeks.org/what-is-data-mining-a-complete-beginners-guide/
- Wiggins, D. (2023, March 7). Speech Recognition & Speech Synbook Glossary (A-G). Omniscien Technologies.
- Wilta, F., Chong, A. L. C., Selvachandran, G., Kotecha, K., & Ding, W. (2022, July). Generalized Susceptible–Exposed–Infectious–Recovered model and its contributing factors for analysing the death and recovery rates of the COVID-19 pandemic. Applied Soft Computing, 123, 108973. https://doi.org/10.1016/j.asoc.2022.108973
- Yagi, M., Yamanouchi, K., Fujita, N., Funao, H., & Ebata, S. (2023, June 21). Revolutionizing Spinal Care: Current Applications and Future Directions of Artificial Intelligence and Machine Learning. Journal of Clinical Medicine, 12(13), 4188. https://doi.org/10.3390/jcm12134188

FSC
www.fsc.org
MIX
Papier | Fördert
gute Waldnutzung
FSC® C083411

Kolibri 360 GmbH
Ferdinand-Jühlke-Straße 7
99095 Erfurt, Deutschland
produktsicherheit@kolibri360.de

Druck:
CPI Druckdienstleistungen GmbH
im Auftrag der
Kolibri 360 GmbH
Ferdinand-Jühlke-Str. 7
99095 Erfurt